CUSTOMER SATISFACTION GUARANTEED

HOW TO ORDER

Quantity discounts are available from the publisher,
Life Education®, Inc.,
Star Route 2-3969G,
Trinity Center, CA 96091
(916) 266-3235

CUSTOMER SATISFACTION GUARANTEED

A New Approach to Customer Service, Bedside Manner, and Relationship Ease

Robert C. Kausen

Life Education,® Inc.
Star Route 2-3969G
Trinity Center, CA 96091
(916) 266-3235

Typography by Life Education®,Inc.

Published in the United States by Life Education, Inc.
Coffee Creek, CA

Publisher Cataloging in Publication Data
Kausen, Robert C.
Customer Satisfaction Guaranteed: A New Approach to Customer Service, Bedside Manner, and Relationship Ease
  1.Customer Relations 2.Customer Service 3.Interpersonal Relations 4. Communications in Organizations
  I. Title
658.812   88-82334
ISBN 0-945787-55-3

91   10 9 8 7 6 5 4 3

DEDICATION

This book is dedicated to all people who serve the public with the hope they may experience the joy inherent in true service.

ABOUT THE AUTHOR

Robert Kausen stumbled into human relations work. He was graduated from the California Institute of Technology as an Applied Chemist. Although he held jobs as sales clerk, salesman, manager, trainer, and consultant, (as well as husband and parent), his primary focus was intellectual. Along the way it became painfully obvious that he knew very little about people. He had become proficient in <u>analyzing</u> personalities and styles but had little <u>understanding</u> for and about people.

In 1976 he switched careers. The chemistry of people became more important than the chemistry of things. Once he began learning about people from the inside out, his life started to simplify and he began to experience the real joy of serving another human being.

Robert decided to write this book because in his work with companies around the world it became clear that most people say they want to treat their employees and customers well. Few understand why they don't. Once you read this book you will probably agree that the human process is by far more challenging and rewarding than any chemical processes.

Table of Contents

TO THE READER

Serving the public is one of the most demanding and, at the same time, rewarding professions. It demands graceful interaction with numerous challenging personalities whose moods may fluctuate from ecstatic to neurotic. You are expected to take in stride harangues, demands, temper tantrums, indecisiveness, and sexual innuendo with the same aplomb as you do a friendly smile or grateful kudos.

Service, on the other hand, is astonishingly rewarding. To be in service requires the ability to look beyond your own needs, likes and dislikes. It demands a level of sturdiness in the world and perspective in life that most people never attain. Without the understanding of and love for people, true service is not possible. But understanding what it takes to be in service is the most marvelous gift you can give yourself. With that understanding, life becomes more effortless, relationships more joyful, and you wake up each morning liking who you are and what you do, feeling grateful to be alive. This book is a beginning look at that understanding.

This manual reveals the dynamics of how people function and shows you how to incorporate commonsense findings about human interaction that are not yet widely recognized. It offers insights into interactions with your customers that will turn toughies into interesting characters, and put you miles ahead on the road to successful customer and job satisfaction.

A suggestion if I may. The point of the book is to increase your commonsense understanding of people, not to convey information. So, relax while you read. The first time through simply read to get the gist, the feeling and sense; don't try to remember anything or let details get in your way. You can always go back and re-read the sections that seem important to you. If you find the book helpful or have any suggestions for improving it, please write to me. I would love hearing from you.

Enjoy your customers and yourself. Satisfaction is guaranteed -- in fact it's built in.

ACKNOWLEDGMENT

It is not possible to acknowledge everyone who has contributed to this book, but there are a few who stand out whom I want to thank especially. First, a man who has opened my eyes at least a little to truth, turned my life upside down, and been an inspired mentor and special friend these past years: Sydney Banks, author of <u>Second Chance</u>, and <u>In Quest of the Pearl</u>.

My colleague and dear friend, George Pransky who is a wellspring of ideas and insights. His contribution to an article in *Restaurants & Institutions* (May 1, 1985) sparked the concept for this book. Third, my best friend and wife Dee Dee who has supported me even in the hard times in my crazy notion to write a book.

The staff at the Advanced Human Studies Institute (Tampa, Florida) have been special teachers for me over these past years. Dr. William Petit, psychiatrist and founder of the Psychiatric Institute of Florida (Braedenton) is a good friend and wonderful therapist.

Pat Tucker is what every would-be author hopes for — an editor who can clean up and clarify without taking over the style.

I would also like to thank several people who read drafts and offered comments: Carol Baskerville, Sue Blondel, Wendy Beckett, Kent Castle, Linda Clough, Mary Kausen, Bill Marvin, Lyn McCright, Jane Neff, Jane Nelsen , Joe San Filippo, and Kraemer Winslow. Special thanks to Trudy Way for the idea which led to the title.

I thank all these wonderful people and especially the thousands of students and clients who are my real teachers.

CUSTOMER SATISFACTION GUARANTEED

1

Why Customer Satisfaction?

Satisfied customers are the life blood of any business.

Why does one retail business flourish while comparable businesses fail? Why do you enjoy dealing with certain establishments and avoid others? What is it beyond actions and words that shapes the customer's experience?

We all know that a successful business must sell its product or services. People will buy a product or service if it fills their need and is priced appropriately, or if it's priced lower, and/or if they like doing business with you. We all know people who buy on impulse (needing to be spontaneous); others who put up with poor quality and service if the price is cheap enough; still others who buy from you regardless of price because they like doing business with you.

Successful businesses stay competitive by offering their customers some kind of extra. Whether the "extra" is tempting displays, cut prices, or good service, <u>every</u> business owner knows (or soon finds out) that taking care of the customer is top priority.

A recent survey by the National Retail Merchants Association pinpoints the reasons retailers lose customers:

> poor attitude of store personnel - 68%
> unadjusted complaints - 14%
> lower prices elsewhere - 9%
> competition, moving or death - 9%

In other words, more than 80% of lost customers are lost because of store personnel's poor people skills. Another study commissioned by the U.S. Office of Consumer Affairs showed that only a third of dissatisfied customers went back to the business that upset them. However, if their complaint was satisfactorily and rapidly resolved, nine out of ten returned.

It is widely accepted that an unhappy customer is likely to tell between six and nine other people about their bad experience, while a satisfied customer may recommend you to only three or four others. Clearly business owners cannot afford those talkative unhappy customers.

Price cutting and dramatic display are standard competition measures, but the basic principles of how to achieve an environment of good service are not widely understood. The once haughty banks have discovered that they can no longer expect customers to walk in; they're busy devising ingenious lures to attract accounts and keep them. Restaurants are re-learning the value of service. Department stores, real estate offices, hairdressing salons, grocery stores, airlines, and even hospitals are all finding that customers care enough about the way they are treated to make the difference between profit and loss.

So the business owner who wants to succeed has the best reason in the world to make sure employees practice positive and effective customer service relations. The results are there in bottom-line profits that govern survival in the competitive market place.

But another dimension is even closer to home for those of us who deal with the public. The enjoyment you yourself get from your work depends on your understanding of people and how they function. When difficult and demanding customers hassle you, your day stretches to agonizing length. Chances are your upset feelings go home with you to ruin your evening as well. But when you handle people with ease and skill, you feel more energy at the end of the day than when you started, and go to sleep looking forward to the next day.

The ancient definition still holds: customer service is taking care of your customers in such a way that they prefer to do business with you. The less well recognized fact is that insisting on mechanical smiles and empty phrases ("Have a good day!") is NOT the effective way to do it. Customer service cannot be faked.

Unless those who serve you really care how customers are treated, their phony friendliness is more apt to irritate than please. And it backfires. Those waiters, clerks and tellers inevitably come to hate their work.

It's easy enough to serve customers well when they are pleasant and know exactly what they want. It's the angry, critical, or undecided customer who tests your skill.

The secret of successful customer service lies not as much in what you do as in how you see people and how you handle the dynamics of the transaction. When you gain a deeper understanding of what's going on you'll find dealing with even the most difficult customer an invigorating opportunity instead of a trial.

Serving nice people is a pleasure, you say, but what about difficult customers? That's when the work becomes hard....

- Successful customer satisfaction is the result of a service state of mind in the employee, and a pro-human relations climate in the organization. Both must have an enlightened perspective.

2

Why Would Anyone Want To Be Difficult?

Compassion and understanding transform difficult personalities into loving people.

Nobody wants to be difficult. If they could see a way out that made sense to them, a way to feel positive and friendly, they would take it. The difficult customer is a prisoner in his or her negative thought system at that moment. Some have been prisoners most of their lives. For customers to be angry, nasty or hurtful towards you, they must be seeing things in a very negative way. In other words, their behavior is just the tip of the iceberg. They are hurting inside and don't know how to escape. In our work with more than 15,000 people we have never found a case where this wasn't true. However, since you may run into difficult people while serving the public, it makes sense to learn how to make these encounters as easy as possible.

Difficult customers have problems, of course, but those problems are <u>theirs</u>. It isn't the customer, but your thoughts and reactions that cause problems. Remember, no one can feel an emotional reaction without first having a triggering thought. When you are angry, your anger starts with a thought. When you are bored -- it's your thought. Fear, resentment, excitement -- whatever the emotion, it starts with a thought.

Suppose a two-year-old child throws a tantrum. He screams and yells at you "I hate you! I hate you!" You would most likely discount the child's behavior and would certainly not take it as a personal assault. You would probably say that this child is upset, and is acting it out. If this same person screams and yells at you thirty years later, you might view that same behavior differently and respond angrily.

The difference is only in what you think. You think that a grown person should know better. The truth is that not all adults know better. Many people feel so insecure that they drop into a negative mood and seek escape by reverting to childish behavior dictated by old thought patterns.

Recently a client, troubled by her husband's anger, heard me say this, and it struck home to her. "That's it!" she burst out. "When my husband gets upset he acts like a two-year-old! I get frightened which makes the situation that much worse. Now I'm ashamed that I've been so blind to his distress."

There is no question that this woman will react differently the next time her husband flies into a rage. In fact, when her reactions become less threatening, his feelings of insecurity and hence his anger will decrease.

Remember the two-year-old, and learn to see what lies behind other people's actions. You needn't look for malice. You are not their target. No one wants to live in negativity. When people fall into that state of mind they may be temporarily "insane." At that moment negative behavior makes total sense to them. Recognize their innocence.[1] They cannot act differently at the moment and they don't even realize what has happened.

When people behave negatively, it's because they don't see any other option. If you can show them a way out, most of them will grab it eagerly.

We repeat that the key to anyone's outlook on life is their state of mind. In the daily fluctuations of your own state of mind, you recognize your moods. What is harder to recognize is that your own thinking is what pulls you into negative moods, changes your logic and dims your experience of life. In a low mood, everything looks more negative. Here is a chart of symptoms that might help you identify lower and higher states of mind.

---

1   I am not suggesting that people are not accountable for their actions. Understanding the true cause of their actions makes it easier to deal with them, leads to better relationships, and helps keep you from reacting negatively.

State of Mind	Feeling Tone	Thoughts/Acts
Higher	Joyful, loving	Compassion Service
	Respectful	Take life in stride
	Irritable	Impatient/Critical Distant
	Defensive	Intolerant Judgmental
Lower	Insecure	Anxious
	Victimized	Self-centered Blame others
	Angry/fearful	Suspicious Belligerent Fight/withdraw

HELIUM PRINCIPLE

One of the most hopeful parts of human functioning is the helium principle. You and everyone else are by nature pulled toward higher states of mind. Whenever you drop the weight of negative thought, your state of mind quite naturally soars to a positive level.

● Human spirits naturally rise.

Suppose when you're at work your manager says, "Betty, I'd like to see you in my office on your lunch break. I have something to discuss with you." You don't know why and you can detect nothing from her neutral tone. Logically, there is nothing for you to do but wait the hour and go to

20

to her office. But nooooooooooooooooo! Your insecurities go to work on your thinking. *I wonder what she wants? Have I done something wrong? I can't imagine what it would be; unless it's about... She can't fire me for something like that. Then again, you never know with her.*

With each such thought your state of mind sinks lower. By the time you reach her office, you are burdened, sullen, and on guard. She starts off with, "I've been noticing your work lately," (Here it comes.) "and I want to tell you that you are doing a terrific job. In fact I am putting you in for a raise." The moment you hear the end of her sentence your thinking does an about-face. The dead weight of negative thought drops away and you zoom up. That's the power of thought in our lives.

● Compassion lubricates human interaction.

When you get a customer who is negative, realize that he or she is in a low state of mind -- the result of feeling insecure. Even though that person's behavior may take the form of bragging, threatening, demanding, or the like, it is driven by insecurity. To find a warm feeling for those people, remind yourself that they are victims of their own thinking. After all you and I have been there many times. Understanding and the warm feelings of compassion will protect your state of mind from triggering your own negative thoughts -- and protect your customer from any impact your negative reactions would otherwise cause.

Imagine a customer walks into your place of business with a hostile air and a scowl that strikes terror in the hearts of most. If you have very little compassion and understanding for this person then you will become insecure and most certainly react with defensive measures, perhaps even growing angry in return.

If you respond with more human feeling and understanding you won't feel defensive, but you might feel puz-

21

zled with this person's manner. You haven't done anything to warrant his behavior, so why is he acting this way?

If you find even deeper feeling then you understand very well what is happening, and your heart goes out to the poor soul. You have a warm feeling for him as a human being, you are able to look past his negativity and recognize someone who is caught in a very low state of mind.

It's hard for people to stay in low states of mind when they are exposed to compassion and understanding. The helium principle is always pulling them up to higher levels.

We presented these principles to several hundred hair stylists in Los Angeles. Only a few weeks later, one of the managers related this incident. A carbon copy of the ogre described above walked into their shop. "In the past when something like this happened, the entire staff cringed," she told me. "Each of us hoped the old grouch would ask for somebody else. But this time was different. We all now recognized what was going on with the unfortunate man. The receptionist welcomed him cheerfully and maintained her warm manner despite his grudging response. The hair stylist simply overlooked his grouchy comments as she cut his hair. Sure enough, her deep feelings of compassion gradually pulled him into a better mood as the helium principle you talked about started working. And do you know that after he paid his bill, he turned and said to everybody 'I really had you people going didn't I? I apologize. I was in a rotten mood when I came in here. You've made a difference and I thank you."

In dealing effectively with difficult people, it's essential to keep the situation in proper perspective....

3

It's Just a Thought

What you think creates reality as you know it.

Flip Wilson used to say "What you sees is what you gets." At one level he simply meant that he doesn't get any better; take him as he is. At a deeper level it touches on the heart of all human experience. That is, what you see via your thinking is what you experience moment to moment. Every person wears a set of glasses or filters made up of their thoughts. Those filters are their personal interpreter of life.

Let's take a few minutes to understand just how people actually experience life's events.

We think. Thinking is an ongoing process that occurs naturally without effort. Like breathing you cannot stop thinking as long as you're alive. Because you have free will, you are able to choose what you think. As a crystal or droplet turns light into a rainbow, your mind converts energy into thought. Whatever enters your senses is translated into experience via thought.

Ever since you were born, you've been collecting a complex array of data. Everything you have read, heard, experienced, seen on TV, listened to on the radio, learned in school, been told by your parents is all recorded in your marvelous brain. The data is stored and used according to an intricate system organized by your values, judgments and beliefs. We call this your thought system. Your reality, everything you experience, is generated by your thought system. In truth, you create the world you live in.

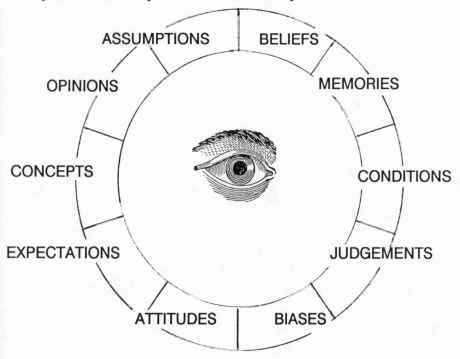

● The human mind produces thought

It is as though you were making the video cassette you are playing. The particular thought combinations you access determine the show you will experience. So in the truest sense each of us generates illusions in our head via thought which we call reality. You project into your own head each scene, each experience. But this show is spectacular because it comes complete with emotions that make it very real.

• Thoughts create emotions making events seem real

Let's say that someone severely criticizes you for something you've done. Your emotional experience will be generated by your thought system at that moment. If you don't understand that it is your thoughts about what happened -- not what happened -- that cause your pain and anger, you may end up feeling victimized by circumstances and people.

Have you ever talked over an experience that made you angry with someone who laughed heartily because to him or her it seemed only funny? And did you see the comic side and begin to view the incident quite differently as a result? The event itself didn't change, but your perception of it, your reality, changed.

A good friend of mine went to an off-beat movie and came out feeling disappointed because the movie missed the mark. He mentioned his opinion to his companion who said, "But that was brilliant satire! Real tongue in cheek humor." They had sat in the same theater for the same two hours but they might as well have seen different films. My friend felt a little foolish; perhaps he'd missed the point. When he reviewed the movie in the light of this new input, he saw that it was indeed a good movie. The external reality had not changed one iota, but his emotional experience had changed substantially because his way of looking at it had changed. This is the power of thought.

Emotions are created by thought. If you feel guilty it's because of judgment thoughts inside your own head about what you did or did not do. (The next time you feel guilty, notice the standard you have violated.) If you resent some-

25

thing it's your own standards, thoughts created in your own mind, that have been violated by someone else. And the same is true of every other emotion you will ever feel. Let's play with an example to make the point.

Imagine you are waiting in line for a department store sale. A man barges right in front of you stepping on your toe. How would you feel? Most of us would be furious. You might grab his shoulder, yank him around and give him a piece of your mind. But what if you notice he's wearing dark glasses and carrying a white cane? Would your anger suddenly change to chagrin? You might feel embarrassed by your first angry reaction. Then suppose the next moment the person behind you says he has seen this guy before. "He really isn't blind. This is a sick game he plays." Now maybe you're really upset. But before you can react someone walks up and says, "Smile, you're on Candid Camera." Your roller coaster of emotions ending in a chuckle was built entirely of what <u>you thought</u> each moment.

Put a wide 18-foot long board on the ground and walk from one end to the other. No big deal, right? Any particular emotional reaction? Aside from wondering why you're even doing such a pointless thing, probably not. Now raise the board twenty feet off the ground and walk the length. You probably experience fear.The fear comes from your thoughts about what might happen if....

I'm not suggesting that fear is always inappropriate. Fear protects you in many cases. The point is to realize that <u>every</u> emotional experience comes from your thought system -- whether or not you can identify the specific thought responsible for the emotion.

If you're in a theater watching the three-dimensional version of "Jaws," you might feel pleasantly excited and scared but you would probably recognize that it was unnecessary to try to protect yourself. Not even when the shark lunges out of the screen at you. Why? Because inside your head you know that it's just a movie, it's not real. If you could maintain that perspective in your day-to-day living, you would find that many difficult circumstances and people are easy to handle. You might still feel the difficulties quite strongly, but you'd know what kind of response would be effective.

Suppose your mate comes home upset and irritable. He or she snaps at you and starts criticizing you. Your feelings are hurt and you are about to lash back. If you realize that it is your thoughts reacting to what your mate is saying and doing that hurt your feelings, you will find a brief moment for perspective. If you can further realize that your mate must be seeing things at the moment through negative thoughts or he/she couldn't be acting this way, then you will know enough to keep quiet and let it pass. You know that lashing out will only make things worse and solve nothing.

There is another factor that makes it more challenging to maintain that "movie" perspective. Even though it's your thinking that creates your emotional experience, the emotional experience created by your thinking affects your state of mind.

● Thought changes your state of mind

In it's small fluctuations you recognize state of mind as change in mood levels. The more positive your mood, the more you understand the impact of your own thinking, and the more positive your experience of reality. You simply can't take negative thoughts too seriously. On the other hand negative moods diminish understanding of the power of thought and make your outlook more negative. Negative thoughts take on great significance.

Imagine you are stuck in traffic on the freeway when a radio news bulletin reports a major accident up ahead and there is no way you can exit. You are stuck in your car for the next hour. Notice in the thinking portrayed in the left-hand column how the driver discounts his negative thoughts and becomes lighter, while the driver in the right-hand column becomes serious and more upset.

Damn. I'll never make my three o'clock appointment. Rotten luck. And this customer is so fussy about time. I'll probably lose the sale.

Damn, it's just my luck. Some stupid driver blew it and ruined it for everybody. There goes my chance to make the sale. I'll never make the three o'clock appointment now and he'll never give me another shot.

Surely he'll understand. After all what can I do. There's no way I can get off the highway.

If I lose this sale, I'll never make quota for the month. All because of some stupid idiot. And just when I'm running late anyway.

Look at the young kid in the next car. It must be nice to just sit there and listen to music. You can bet he doesn't have an appointment to keep. Or if he does, he's sure relaxed about it.

I'll never get ahead in this company. There's always some obstacle in the way. I never get any help from my boss and he always assigns me the toughest prospects.

Don't kids have anything better to do than clog the highways and play loud music. No wonder the world is in such bad shape. Guess I'll turn on the news.

Guess I'll listen to the radio too. Might as well relax. I'm not going anywhere. What am I going to tell my customer? I need that sale. Oh well, worrying about it is just going to get me more upset.

This has been a hectic day. I should not try to cram so much into so few hours. Say, this music isn't bad

Hey that's interesting. I wonder if those two women knew each other or just struck up a conversation. It's a traffic jam party.

What AM I going to do about my three o'clock appointment? Say maybe I'll get out of my car and meet some people. Maybe somebody has a car phone and I can call my customer. It's a great excuse to pass the time with people

What's the point anyway. The national debt keeps growing, taxes get worse, terrorists are calling the shots.

I'm sure bored with my marriage. The nag hasn't changed in fifteen years.

Get this line moving. Can't the police do anything right?

Women have it easy. Look at those two. Nothing to do but stand around and talk. It doesn't matter to them if they are delayed. But I've got important things to do. Damn!

As you start understanding this relationship between thought, reality, and state of mind in your daily life you will find yourself less trapped by negative thoughts.

Here is another way to look at it. Picture your moods as an elevator -- one of those mounted on the exterior of a tall hotel so you can see the outside view as you move up and down. The elevator operator is your thinking. Insecure thoughts punch the buttons to lower levels while the unconditional, positive feelings take you to higher levels. As you look out from the elevator at different levels the reality out there doesn't change, but your view -- the reality you experience -- changes. At the lowest levels you may see only dirt, debris and tree trunks. At higher levels you may see the entire countryside and a beautiful sunset. This is how moods work.

Now place the hotel on the side of a mountain. If it is located near the bottom of the mountain your view is limited no matter how high your mood. If the hotel is moved up the hill your overall perspective improves. This is level of consciousness. The hill represents your level of understanding, insight into the function of thought, or innate wisdom. As this grows in your life your low moods are no longer as low and your high moods bring you even greater insight and perspective.

Your understanding becomes common sense to you. Your level of consciousness -- the depth at which you instinctively understand how thought creates reality -- permanently shifts and your range of moods becomes more positive. You don't feel permanently lost in low moods; you know they will pass. More and more you will enjoy an exhilarating sense of unconditional well being. This is true self-esteem.

Now let's take a look at how to go about dropping distractions, those unwanted, nonfunctional thoughts....

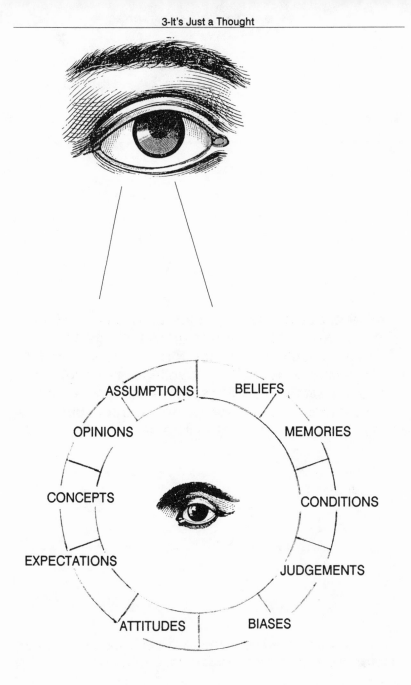

●**Common sense provides perspective on 'reality'.**

● Deep, positive feelings inherently reside within each person. When these feelings are experienced in their pure form, life is simple and meaningful. When these feelings are polluted by personal thought, life appears complicated and life's meaning must be contrived from subjective thought systems.*

* This and other Corollaries of Common Sense appearing at the end of some chapters were co-authored by Dr. George Pransky.

4
—

Presence

Presence is the power behind satisfaction.

Just suppose that someone offered you a product guaranteed to accomplish the following:

¤   Bring out the best in other people without requiring you to memorize techniques or remember theories

¤   Significantly reduce if not eliminate the pressure and effort in your work

¤   Bring you deep job satisfaction, regardless of the nature of your work

¤   Positively impact others

¤   Enrich your professional and personal relationships

¤   Ensure professional success and evolution on a daily basis

¤   AND, cost you nothing!

We are talking about PRESENCE. People who have high presence are often described as charismatic, engaging, inspiring, attractive, and caring, or as having a good bedside manner, high impact, natural ability, or an engaging manner.

Presence is natural, yet rare. If we are all born with presence (ever seen a baby without it?), then why isn't everyone charismatic and impactful?

The answer is that presence can be, and usually is, diminished in the process of growing up. Presence is simply your capacity to stay in the moment without distractions; to be present as life is happening.

$$\frac{\text{Span of AWARENESS} - \text{DISTRACTIONS}}{= \text{PRESENCE}}$$

That's the formula that produces the magic product described above. Each of us has a certain span of awareness or natural impact. To maximize your presence, you simply drop distractions. Sound easy? It is.

● Presence is the absence of distractions

Customer satisfaction has nothing to do with gimmicks or slogans. It is what happens naturally when you are right there with your customer (no distracting thoughts in your head) -- when you have high presence.

If you are with a friend or mate, don't you instantly know when he or she is preoccupied with something else? When

Dad comes home from a busy day at the office, the children can always tell whether he is really home or still has his head back at the office. A friend was flying a kite after work with his three-year- old daughter. Innocently she asked: "Daddy, when are you coming home?" "I am home," he said irritably, "I'm right here." "No I mean really home, Daddy!" she insisted with unnerving innocence.

● Everyone senses a distracted mind

Presence is the state of giving your full attention to the matter at hand. Customers quickly sense the difference, if only on a subconscious level. For example, if you are waiting on a customer but thinking about your lunch break, last night's party, or the tip you hope to get, your presence is automatically lowered -- and the customers feel vaguely cheated. They may not know why but they feel it, and your place of work loses some of its attraction.

You don't have to do anything to develop presence; you already have it. But distracting thoughts in your head hide it from your customers. When you begin to exclude distracting thoughts you automatically achieve higher presence.

People are constructed with two major sources of thinking. One is the analytical/ memory source which we use for recalling information, planning, judging, worrying, etc. When a person is distracted, too busy, over-whelmed, upset, this is the source of thinking -- and it takes away from presence. The other source of thinking is inspiration/contemplation. When a person is operating in this mode they have high presence and are acclaimed super listeners.

Merely accepting that it's good business to have more presence starts the process.

Beyond the boost presence gives to your business is the personal reward. When you are present with your customers, you feel better. Operating with distractions in your head is like riding a bike with the brakes on. It makes your work so much harder that you are worn out. You lose the thrill of freedom and ease in living and your distractions make you feel alone and separate from people.

To gain more presence, start to <u>disrespect</u> the distracting thoughts and <u>respect</u> the quieter, peaceful state of mind. When you notice that you are distracted simply acknowledge that to yourself and realize that you are better off with fewer thoughts in your head. As you begin to naturally quiet down, be grateful for it. Your gratitude will bring you even more presence.

Let's look at some of these distractions, these hindering thoughts....

5

Dropping Distractions

Distractions are like sand with gold; they come with the pay load but detract from the value.

High presence is the absence of distracting thoughts. The key to increasing presence is learning to drop the distractions that diminish your natural presence. The major categories of distractions are:

¤ differences between unique thought systems;

¤ reactions to mood changes;

¤ nonfunctional thoughts -- those that work against you.

These all occur quite naturally, but deeper understanding will make it a lot easier for you to drop distractions whenever they start to get in the way and lower your presence.

Separate Cultures

When you travel in a hot country such as Mexico, you find that virtually every shop closes for two or three hours after lunch for the siesta. It doesn't matter how much money you may want to spend or how important your business is, their doors are closed. If someone did that in the United States you might say they were unmotivated. In Mexico, you smile and tell yourself that this is how they do it here.

In some parts of Europe when you arrive at work each morning, you shake hands with everyone in the place. For us it seems absurdly formal, but in that culture it's how things are done.

When U.S. business people started doing business with the Japanese after World War II they were astonished and frustrated to find no Japanese was willing to get down to business for several days after first making contact. The Americans soon discovered that the Japanese consider it rude to discuss business until the proper relationship and ambiance have been established. Once Americans dropped their judgments about the cultural differences, they began to learn the wisdom of conducting business Japanese style. After you have reached a level of trust with a Japanese businessman, he will bind himself to and execute multi-million-dollar deals on the strength of a handshake alone. The Japanese know that the strength of an agreement rests on understanding and trust and not on pieces of paper.

Years ago, when I was stationed in Germany, my wife and I entertained several German couples in our home. We both noticed that all the smokers were raiding our American cigarettes. For half the evening we were annoyed that they would take such advantage of our hospitality. Then a friend took us aside and explained that the German custom is for the host to provide the cigarettes, that in fact it's considered impolite for guests to smoke their own. Of course, our irritation promptly evaporated. Understanding changed our thinking.

If you go where the culture and customs of the country are different, you expect to allow for unfamiliar behavior. It helps to think of each human being as a unique "culture." A person's culture is simply the particular combination of values, beliefs, standards, ethics, and morals that make up that person's thought system. It is as unique as a fingerprint. Each person's unique "culture" determines that person's behavior. So in the truest sense, you can no more afford to fault another's manner when you find it obnoxious than to fault the siesta custom. Their manner is "how they do things."

● Everyone sees life in a unique way

To illustrate how differently people see things, imagine three separate people looking for a used car. Let's say all three come to look over a 1956 Chevy. Each one is looking through a different set of filters (thoughts) so each one sees the car in a different way. (Everybody looks through negative thoughts in a low state of mind and positive thoughts in a high state of mind.) Mr. A sees a classic collector's piece. He pictures it in showroom condition, painted in the classic two-tone white and aquamarine. He sees sparkling chrome bumpers and trim, and brand new whitewall tires. He can already feel his pride as he drives it around town on a Sunday afternoon. Even after all the repairs and restoration, he knows this showpiece will increase in value with time and prove to be an excellent investment.

Looking at the same vehicle, Mr. B sees a sturdy car that might make do as a third car for the family. The rusty areas don't seem to affect it structurally and when the oxidized paint is polished up it will look quite decent. If it runs well, he'll consider it -- at the right price.

Mr. C. sees a junker. A 30-year-old car means to him breakdowns and repairs. He looks underneath and spots the oil drops he expected to find. This clunker would require plenty of dollars in repairs, and even then would be only a 30-year-old car to him. He thinks no one in his right mind would even consider such a bad investment.

The difference between these three views is the difference between three thought systems. Each person could talk extensively with airtight logic to support his view. A thought system is always internally and externally self-validating.

So who is right? Of course, they are all right. Each of them is operating from his own consistent thought system. By definition, that is being right.

You have probably guessed by now that A,B, and C could also be the same person in three different states of mind. This is because a low state of mind shifts your thinking to a more negative logic. The essential thing to note is that these differences are not limited to cars, but show up in most of your life experiences.

● State of mind produces consistent logic.

At home, Mr.A (who saw the collector's show piece) is likely to experience (see) his family as positive and fun. His children are a source of joy and delight. Their loud times and the messes they get into are just part of growing up. On the other hand Mr. C (who could only see a junker) finds chaos and negativity wherever he goes. His kids drive him crazy and his house seems to be in a constant state of turmoil.

In presenting this example to a class of 11 to 13 year-olds, we asked them whether they thought the behavior of Mr. C's children was actually different from that of Mr. A's or was just perceived as different. Most of them were sure that the only difference was in the perception. A few felt there must be actual behavioral differences. Both opinions may be true, but the perception is the key, since the way a child is perceived does change the child's behavior. When children are seen as unruly, untrustworthy, or irresponsible they usually begin to see themselves that way as well and act accordingly. We tend to get what we expect out of life. We do, indeed, create our own reality.

● It's all in the eye of the beholder

On a camping trip Mr. A finds nature a peaceful, soul-satisfying refuge from the hustle of his usual business day. He revels in the clean air, pure mountain water, and beautiful skies. He finds himself back in touch with what counts in life. The absence of TV, radio, and telephone is a welcome break from his normal ties with life. As he relaxes in the sun he feels more and more like he has come back home.

Mr. C is quite another story. He first notices the dirt everywhere, the lack of modern conveniences. The ground is hard, the sun too hot and the nights too cold. He is restless and bored before the end of the first day, and begins to wonder why he agreed to spend a whole weekend. The flies, mosquitoes and ants tell him that he has been deprived of the good life.

● Everyone creates their own experience

At work the two men will very likely experience just as many differences because thought systems are consistent. After all, each still views the world through his unique thought system. Mr. A loves his work and finds each day filled with surprises and opportunities for creativity. He enjoys having problems thrown his way because they offer him an opportunity to be creative. He is always surprised

41

when he glances up to see that hours have raced by without his even noticing.

Mr. C, of course, sees things in a much more negative way. He doesn't like his job much, feels unappreciated, and finds himself bored with the work, which he considers beneath his capabilities. It seems to him that everyone is bent on creating more problems just to complicate his day. His clock must have a malfunction; it certainly stretches out the minutes more than anyone else's.

These are extreme examples, but look around at your friends and see if you don't notice a consistency in the way they view various parts of their lives. The perfectionist does nothing well enough. The critic finds something wrong everywhere. The worrier always worries whether there is anything to worry about or not.

It's not that one way of viewing life is correct or another wrong. The point is that everyone sees life, and thus experiences life, in an individual way that makes each person's reality unique and different from the reality of every other person on earth.

<u>Understanding that each person has created a different reality in his or her mind is a major step in getting along easily with people.</u>

When you resent someone's behavior, opinions, or beliefs you automatically erect a barrier at the feeling level which normally provides the innate connection we call closeness, or connectedness. If, instead of judging the other person's thought system, you look at that person as a unique culture, the differences become a source of interest and learning. You find yourself eager to discover more about their customs and their way of seeing the world. Their idiosyncrasies become endearing. You can get some of the pleasure of foreign travel just by exploring the people you meet every day.

Since each of us lives in a unique culture, we will appreciate and enjoy other people only if we try to understand their unique view of the world. If you don't know this, then of course you imagine that there is only one true reality, one right way. Guess whose?

Arguments, fights and wars arise from lack of this understanding. When you understand that the customer has a unique view, you won't feel the urge to change it or make him wrong. You'd have as much success with that as you would if you tried to eliminate the Mexican siesta, stop the French from drinking wine, or the Germans from shaking hands.

Changing Moods

Each of us goes through mood swings every day. Some feel they are chained to a roller coaster while others seem to stay fairly constant. A mood swing is nothing more than a shift in our understanding of the role of thought.

In a good mood, everything looks positive and you are full of hope. You see opportunities instead of problems, possibilities instead of limitations, and you meet interesting characters rather than difficult people. In this wiser state of mind your thinking tends to be functional; that is, you appreciate the role of thought in shaping your reality. If a negative thought floats into your head, you see it as just a crazy thought, or at least as highly suspect. Your thinking tends to serve your needs and lead you to even more positive feelings.

In a bad mood, everything looks gloomy and negative. You see problems, feel limited, find the world in league against you. Nothing goes right. Clothes don't fit, styles don't suit you, movies are boring, and people are a bother. In this lower state your thinking is nonfunctional. You lose sight of the power of your thinking, you feel victimized.

Negative thoughts are "just the way it is." The lower your mood sinks, the more problems and difficulties you recognize. Everything looks like the tip of a threatening iceberg. In the following example of a man being fired from his management position, the left-hand column represents the thinking in a low state of mind thinking. The right column represents the thinking of the same person in a high state of mind.

Good lord, fired! After all I've done for this organization! I've sweat blood helping to build this company into what it is today, and this is the thanks I get. What'll I do? I don't have enough money saved to last long.

Just because I wasn't willing to play politics like the rest of those brown noses. I knew he really didn't like me -- what a hypocrite, pretending all these years.

I'm ruined. Who wants to hire someone who was fired? Nobody wants a failure. How will I pay the bills? What will I tell my family?

Good lord, fired! After all I've done for this organization! I've sweat blood helping to build this company into what it is today, and this is the thanks I get. (Stunned silence)

Of course! What else could he do? That's great. For the past year I've been trying to steer the company in the opposite direction from the president's. If I were in his position I'd do the same thing.

The truth is I haven't had the courage to strike out on my own. This is obviously the perfect opportunity -- even if it is a little dramatic.

What I'll do is borrow some money and start my own

*company. This is exciting --
and a little scary. But I
know it will work out.*

Before you decide that this is unrealistic, let me confide that the person is me. I started down that dark spiral of negative, victim-role thinking and then it hit me. I did not think my way out of it. I stopped for a moment of silence, let my spirits soar, and had an insight. The rest is history, as they say.

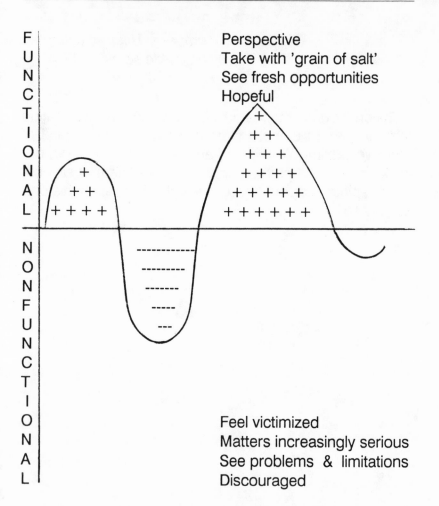

Perspective
Take with 'grain of salt'
See fresh opportunities
Hopeful

Feel victimized
Matters increasingly serious
See problems & limitations
Discouraged

● State of mind determines what thinking you use

When a customer in a low mood comes to you, or if you are in a low state yourself, the yellow caution signals are up. If you are both in a negative state of mind, the red flashing lights should warn you of potential disaster. The key is to recognize what is happening but not to take it too seriously. A person in a low mood is going to be gruff and grouchy. If you are in a low state of mind you are over-sensitive to comments of others. When you recognize the con-

condition, you are better able to maintain perspective and handle the situation.

Recognizing the impact of low moods is the first step. One thing I have learned from personal experience is that fighting a low mood in yourself or someone else is an invitation for it to stick around. It's like the African monkey trap.

To catch a monkey, African trappers put food in a hollow gourd with an opening just large enough to let the monkey slip an open paw in, and chain the gourd to a tree. The monkey reaches in, grabs the food and then cannot remove his fist. The monkey can escape only by relaxing it's paw and letting the food go.

A low mood operates the same way. If you grab it — even if your intention is to demolish it — you can't get free of it. You merely aggravate the negativity, and the mood hangs on or gets worse.

The way to get free of a negative mood is to acknowledge it but not take it seriously. Realize it is just a "brain seizure" of insecure thought. Here's an example of an internal dialogue in this direction. Remember, it's the feelings behind the thoughts that count, not the content. On the left is the negative, frightened part of the brain talking. On the right is that small voice of sanity trying to bring perspective and understanding.

What'll I do? The IRS demands $10,000 for back taxes. I can't believe they disallowed those deductions. It was perfectly legal. I'm ruined. I'll never be able to handle this.

Now wait, that's crazy. Don't listen to those fearful thoughts.

Yes, but the fact is they do want the money and I haven't got it. This is serious.

If you don't have it they can't get it. Stop a moment, calm down. Panic won't solve anything.

Insecure thinking drags you down. Your only hope of finding sensible solutions is to drop insecurity and look for inspiration.

Hmmm. That makes sense. Actually the attorney said that this isn't final yet. He also said they will arrange payments I can handle. I guess they don't want to ruin people just get what's due.

State of mind can be likened to the king-of-the-mountain game we used to play as kids. Normally, good feeling is king. Under certain conditions, negativity can knock good feeling out of its dominant position.

Unlike the game, there is no need to fight a negative mood that is dominating the moment. Simply ignoring or even just discounting negativity will cause it to fall away, and good feelings will again be king. This is true for you as an individual and true when serving customers.

● **Positive state of mind will ultimately prevail**

If you deal with customers whose mood is down, you need only recognize that their negativity is the result of the insecurity that accompanies a low state of mind. You don't have to react to or fight their low mood -- or your own, for that matter. With a little patience, understanding, and human feeling, a more positive mood will return. Reminding yourself of this allows you to be much more understanding and compassionate -- which will, in turn, help to lighten the customer's mood.

Nonfunctional Thoughts

Nonfunctional thoughts, you will recall, are simply thoughts that do not serve you at the moment. They become distractions, they lower your state of mind, and they decrease your presence. Today's nonfunctional thought may be functional at some other time where it has a purpose and serves you at that moment.

Nonfunctional thoughts come in any shape and form. Here are several categories to help you recognize them when they intrude on your peace of mind.

Judgments, evaluations, criticisms

In matters of the heart (relationships of any kind) judgmentalism can only get in the way. It forms a barrier between you and your customer. So when you are relating with people and want that human connection, let go of your judgments of them -- no matter how well justified they may be.

- **Judgments, evaluations, criticisms impair the human connection**

It's not always wrong to judge. If you are shopping for clothes for yourself, you must put on your evaluation glasses to decide what looks right on you. But judgmentalism is another matter. Of course you must use your best judgment in order to determine what you can do for your customers, but to pass judgment on them as personalities according to your own value system is no help at all.

A friend of mine, Tom, decided to go shopping for a car. He was wearing blue jeans and a T shirt. The head salesman made a quick judgment that this customer could not possibly afford the expensive Mercedes Benz he was admiring, and proceeded to ignore Tom. A salesman who regularly seized chances to improve his skills eagerly approached Tom. He took Tom for a test drive and even went with him to Tom's house on the other side of town so Tom's wife could see the car too.

Tom is, in fact, a wealthy man. He wound up buying not only that car but a second one for his wife as well. The senior salesman back at the store got a blunt reminder of the old saw "You can't tell a book by it's cover," and, let's hope, learned something about his own attitude toward his job and his customers.

More often than not our judgments become blinders that hide opportunity from us. I can't tell you how many times I have made an instant judgment about someone or something -- that this person or situation was not worth my time or attention -- only to find out later that I had missed out on an extraordinary opportunity to meet and know a wonderful person. The point is simply to be willing to keep yourself open to possibilities.

Analysis, comparison, strategy

● **When you listen to your thoughts, you can't hear the customer.**

Preoccupation with analyzing your own thoughts and planning your strategies will also lower your presence, and will keep you from being able to really listen to your customer. It is listening at a deep, non-judgmental level that allows you to sense what a customer wants and know how to respond effectively. Others can always tell when you are not really listening. You tend to cut off their sentences, respond from your preconceptions, and you have a hard-edged manner.

When you are really listening, they can tell that you are taking in what they say without passing judgment on them. A true listener hangs on every word. All sales techniques in the world will not take the place of genuine listening.

● Insecurity, self-doubt in you produces doubt in the customer.

If you have ever dealt with a doctor who is insecure around people you know what that means. His insecurity comes across as incompetence, even if you have been told he is a great authority in the field. It is his distracting self-doubt that reduces his presence and blocks the human connection between you. The left column is a dialogue between a patient and a doctor with poor bedside manner; the right column is the same patient with a doctor who has a way with people.

P. (anxious) How serious is this operation, Doctor?
Dr. (clinically) Every operation is serious. Historically the rate of success is better than 80% for this procedure.
P.(scared) You mean there's a one in five chance I won't survive?

P. (anxious) How serious is this operation, Doctor.?
Dr. (compassionate) The most important thing is for you to get well. The problems you've been having in the past few months are all caused by this. When we get it taken care of you're going to feel like a new person.

_Dr._ _(formal, aloof) Don't worry, you are healthy and should do fine._

_P._ _(more frightened) Well I don't know if I like those odds. Maybe I'll get another opinion._

_Dr._ _(defensive) Very well, you can do as you wish. But if you want me to perform the surgery you'll need to let me know soon. I'm quite busy._

_P._ _(hostile) Just how many of these operations have you done, Doctor, and how many of your patients have survived?_

_P._ _(concerned) But how risky is it?_

_Dr._ _(understanding) Well, no surgery is to be taken lightly. We want to operate only when it's absolutely necessary. In this case I do feel it is appropriate and with your excellent health there should be no problems._

_P._ _(uncertain) Is there no alternative to the surgery? I'm feeling nervous about it._

_Dr._ _(warm, reassuring) That's natural. In my opinion, this is the route to take. However, I recommend that you get a second opinion so you will feel confident about what we are doing. I'll be glad to provide the names of several other fine surgeons._

_P._ _(reassured) I think I will do that, Doc, but if surgery is necessary I'll want you to do it. I feel confidence in you._

The warm human feelings of compassion and true understanding (love if you will) have a powerful, almost magical impact on people. When these feelings are strong, we give people the benefit of the doubt, trust implicitly, and listen openly. These feelings -- which we've been calling presence, charisma, or bedside manner — cannot be faked. The good news is they already exist inside everyone. Dropping distractions and limiting thoughts allows these deeper feelings to be present naturally. It's that simple.

<u>Reactions</u>

● Reactions and ill feelings block the human connection

Sometimes it's hard not to respond in kind to what people say or do, hard not to let their unthinking comments or mannerisms dictate your reaction. Some people even seem to specialize in playing games with others' reactions. When people say or do things that get to you, they are only doing what their automatic reactions prescribe in the circumstances.

The key is to recognize that your reactions are just that; <u>your</u> thoughts, not their actions, determine your reaction. They cannot draw you into their reality unless you accept the invitation. You can maintain your full presence, be there with them, without yielding control of your own mood and behavior.

To increase your presence simply note that you are thinking distracting thoughts, then drop them.

To give you a sense of what this means, let's walk through an internal dialogue with a flight attendant who has just been belittled by a male chauvinist. Remember, this is not a technique, so only the flavor is important. The left-hand column is her reactive, insecure thought system talking; the right-hand column is her common sense.

Who is he calling honey?
That burns me up. Who
does he think I am.   *Relax, mellow out. You*
                                          know how these road-worn

salesmen are. He doesn't mean any disrespect.

Yes, but I get so tired of being treated like an object. Why can't customers just treat me like a human being?

Remember all behavior results from the level of understanding and the unique thought system of the individual. He must say what he does, given the way he sees the world. The object here is to keep from getting dragged into his negative world through your reactions.

It still isn't right, his treating me that way.

Right just means to operate in consistence with your thought system. That is exactly what he is doing. So he is <u>right</u>. This is not about being right but about being able to serve this customer and enjoy your job. Just find a little understanding for this person and let warm feelings guide you.

Well , that makes sense but it isn't easy with some people. I'll see what I can do.

Be grateful. He is pointing out an area where you are

*over-sensitive. See him as
a teacher. Do the best you
can and you may see him
change through compas-
sion.*

If it makes sense for you to have as much presence as possible, you will begin to notice the distractions, and drop them as you go along.

Recently one of our clients decided that she wasn't doing well. "I can see that I'm distracted, and I certainly don't want to be," she said. "But it seems to me I'm getting worse."

We pointed out that her feeling was the first sign that her understanding was getting better, not worse. "The fact that you notice your distractions more than ever," we told her, "means that your tolerance for your own busy mind has lessened. This will automatically make you more aware of your own distracting thoughts. You'll soon learn to drop more of them." To determine the inherent noise in a stereo system, you turn the record and tuner off. Then you turn the amplifier volume up to make the noise louder so you can identify the source of any noise; only after that can you deal with it. Our client had turned up the "noise" in her system and was ready for the next step.

Presence leads to a bonus for you....

- **Worry is a negative thought focused on past or future events. It is a habit that serves no positive purpose and in fact limits a person's abilities. It takes hold most rapidly when spirits are low.**

6

Getting Involved

The deeper the involvement, the freer the mind, the greater the joy.

You might ask why all the fuss about customer satisfaction. After all can't you serve customers without worrying about your head? Isn't all this good advice just a way for the company to make more money? True, if you have more presence and the customer experiences better service, it will help business, maybe even get you a raise. But there's a lot more in it for you than that.

The more presence you have, the more involved you are, the more fun you get out of your work. The more distracted you are, the more your performance and enjoyment of your work suffer.

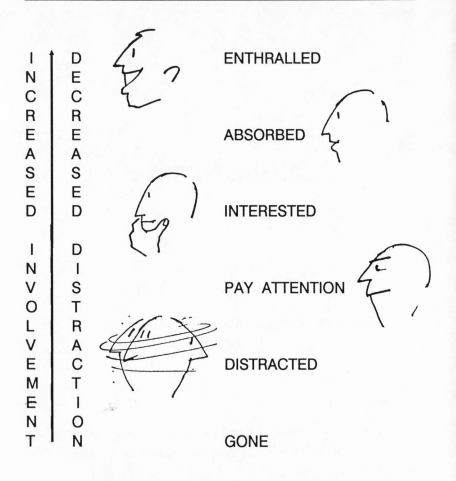

I N C R E A S E D   I N V O L V E M E N T

D E C R E A S E D   D I S T R A C T I O N

ENTHRALLED

ABSORBED

INTERESTED

PAY ATTENTION

DISTRACTED

GONE

● Involvement leads to satisfaction.

In the chart above let's say you are Distracted. These are the times when you are so preoccupied with something else that you literally can't keep your mind on what you're doing. This often happens when you are feeling insecure, when perhaps a traumatic event has invaded your life. As you know, that's when time drags; you resent having to be where you are. That resentful, angry feeling is the price of your distracting thoughts.

When one of my supervisors came dragging in one morning, her normal light manner turned irritable and edgy, I watched her for an hour or so, then drew her aside and asked what was going on. She admitted that her small son had broken out with measles. Out of her dedication to her job, she had made the decision to come in, but she simply was not able to stay present, so I sent her to be with her son.

In a highly distracted state of mind, anyone's performance is poor. If you were playing baseball, you'd probably miss the ball because it would look so tiny and come at you fast. You might even be surprised to discover that while you're still waiting for the pitch the ball was already in the catcher's mitt. When you're distracted, customers are only an imposition and bother. You may even decide you are in the wrong business and take some ill-considered action. Your painful thoughts make it impossible to enjoy your work.

By learning to drop distracting thoughts, most of us can easily bring ourselves to a Pay Attention level. That's an improvement but here you are still easily distracted and have to make a conscious effort to re-focus on the matters at hand. Customers get your divided attention.

They will most likely go away feeling that while you completed the transaction adequately, you felt they were a bother. In baseball, you feel lucky to be able to get a hit since the ball whizzes past at breakneck speed. These days drag so that you feel worn out even when you haven't had that much to do. Your effort to pay attention takes the fun out of the job.

When you learn to quiet distracting thoughts more effectively, you will find yourself becoming Interested. Although you can still be distracted (by the ring of a telephone, the sudden heated discussion across the room, and the like) operating at this level of presence does not drain your energy. Time moves along nicely -- it's not an issue -- and you find whatever you are doing quite pleasant. If you are playing softball, you are really involved in the game; you can easily keep track of the ball, and even hit it. On the job, because you bring them more presence, customers will feel good about their dealings with you. At this level you begin to find ease in your work because the job is no longer a burden.

As you drop off more of those distracting thoughts, you will naturally find yourself with greater presence, becoming Engaged in the moment. These are the days when time flies as you finish up one job after another. Your work day is over before you know it, but you feel more energetic than when you started. Somehow, removing the burden of distracting thoughts is like shedding a ten-ton load. You shift into overdrive and could keep going forever. Or, if it's baseball, you'll find the ball seems to have slowed down so it's much easier to hit.

When asked how he could hold the record for the most home runs and the most strike-outs, Babe Ruth used to say "It's simple to hit the ball when it looks the size of a watermelon coming across the plate. At other times, though, it's more like an aspirin." Professional athletes in top form talk of watching the seams of the ball in flight.

Serving customers at this level is a real treat. There's a certain magic about it. You find yourself tuned in so that it's easy for you to understand and get along with them. In fact it's as if you are friends. You may even become so involved that nothing short of the crash of a tray full of dishes can tear your attention away. Your customers will feel that they are the only ones in the room, and they'll be eager to to tell others about the excellence of the service. Your enjoyment soars because there are few distracting thoughts in your head.

Recently we coached a group of more than a thousand hairdressers along these lines. During the months that followed they reported that not only did the percentage of dissatisfied customers decrease, but referrals and tips went up significantly. The customer-service feeling in the air made the difference.

As your presence increases, so does the quality of your own experience. Eventually you may find yourself so involved that you feel Enthralled. Friends with computers have told me that when they sit down at the keys for a few minutes, they are often astonished to find that in those "few minutes" several hours have gone by. At this level professional athletes talk about "riding with the ball." Time seems to stand still. Time is completely relative, expanding and contracting based on your level of involvement and state of mind.

When interacting with the public, this level is incredibly rewarding. The customers you serve at this high level will feel privileged and grateful. Chances are they'll seek you out every time they come back. It's times like these that make us thankful we have a job that involves people. At these moments, your job is a source of such great joy that you may even be surprised you get paid for doing it.

Distracting thoughts determine the difference between all these levels of presence. When you begin to eliminate distracting thoughts you head in the direction of a quieter mind that leads to an ever richer experience of people, your work, and yourself. There is no end to the possibilities because there's no end to how quiet your mind can become.

Let's take a look at what it takes to be confident and professional with people....

61

● Stress is nothing more than the weight of thought and emotion on the human mind. Thought is the only cause of stress. Circumstances and events are never the cause of stress but merely the triggers for thought.

7

Confidence and Professionalism

Confidence based on external results is like a house built on shifting sands.

When you deal with craft, trade, or professional people you end up with different impressions about their level of confidence and professionalism. One airline attendant can serve you dinner and give you the feeling that your are confidently well cared for, while another, going through exactly the same motions leaves you wondering if he knew what he was doing. One bank teller handling your transaction can make it seem easy, while another leaves you wondering if this is her first day on the job.

Your customers also form impressions. Whether your customer ends up feeling you are a pro or a bush-leaguer depends heavily on your mental state.

Confidence is the nice feeling of well-being you have <u>*before*</u> *you indulge your ego with thoughts of other concerns and self-doubt.* You feel you know what you are doing -- that is, you are not in doubt.

● Confidence is a state of mind

A close friend who successfully conducted a number of self-improvement seminars had so few doubts in her head that most of her students assumed she was at least a PhD psychologist if not a psychiatrist; (she's never even studied psychology -- she just has a lot of common sense.) One day she showed me the ultimate testimonial -- a law suit in which she and the officers of the company were named. One of the allegations was that all of them -- with the possible exception of my friend -- were practicing psychology without a license. Although they were not guilty, this was a great example of how the natural feelings of well-being spell confidence.

A common prescription people apply when they are in doubt is to grit their teeth and tell themselves that they can do it. This is "psyching up" or positive thinking. There are two pitfalls in this approach. First, it doesn't come across as real to anyone -- especially not to you. Second, it is one more set of thoughts to keep in your head and inhibit your presence. It's like feeling burdened while carrying a sack of stones and deciding that you need to balance the load by picking up another sack for the other hand.

The natural state for all of us is a nice sense of well-being. We were born that way. So fortunately, confidence is not something we have to develop. It is a natural feeling, but it can be smothered by negative thoughts of inadequacy, "can't," worry, and concern. As we grow up we often mistakenly make decisions about ourselves based on outer world results and opinions. We begin to allow the judgment of others to override our innate well-being.

My second grade teacher looked down at my drawing of a farm and stated matter-of-factly "You can't draw." Up to that moment I had no concept of my ability — I just enjoyed doing it. I did not feel bad about her statement, I simply recorded it as a fact. (After all, she was twenty feet tall and knew everything.) In the following years I simply avoided drawing since I knew I couldn't. When I was 23, my father-in-law, a famous cartoonist and artist, invited me to paint with him at a nearby fishing wharf. Naturally, my flawless thought record instantly came up with

"I can't draw."

He laughed and assured me that everyone has at least a thousand bad drawings in them and the sooner you get them out the sooner you get to the good ones. I went, I sketched, I enjoyed.

An old friend came to me for help in preparing for a job interview. The sales job he wanted required confidence, and he was having serious doubts about his qualification. "I was fired from my last job because people didn't feel I knew what I was talking about," moaned Malcom. "I'm just not sure how to explain that so they'll give me a chance to prove myself." As Malcom talked it was apparent that he was trying to figure out how to talk himself into feeling better about his past failure.

"Malcom," I said, "none of that matters. That's all history. You've worried yourself into a low state of mind where you are now filled with doubt and concern. Your depressed state is just those dumb thoughts running around in your head. What the interviewer will be looking for is a sense or feeling from you. He may ask questions about why you left that job. If you can understand that back then you fell into the trap of doubting yourself and then having to prove

65

self to others, you'll pop out of this. The moment you realize it, you will feel a surge of positive feelings."

And in fact during that hour we talked it happened. In his more positive state of mind, Malcom was able to abandon his self-doubt and proceed with confidence.

Most people have the misguided notion that confidence is about actions -- techniques, skills. Look around at the fields of law or medicine. All of the practitioners have passed rigorous tests designed to insure that they are technically competent, yet in each field you run into people who just don't seem to know what they are doing. It's not competence that varies as much as the range of confidence. The lack of confidence comes from their thoughts of doubt -- usually their doubts about their ability to deal with people.

CONFIDENCE
+ TECHNICAL PROFICIENCY
_____
= PROFESSIONALISM

You can increase your level of professionalism by increasing either element. You can increase your technical proficiency by finding ways to improve what you do. Increased confidence naturally happens when you start to dismiss your negative thoughts and stop indulging your self-doubts.

Larry Bird of the Boston Celtics is a great example of someone who has done both really well. Bird has been elected Most Valuable Player several times. He is considered by many to be the best all around player in professional basketball. He never rests on those laurels and in fact doesn't seem to pay much attention to them. Before every game he spends more time practicing shots than anyone else. He works constantly on making more and more difficult shots. When his shooting is hot, he works on rebounds or assists. As far as he is concerned, he has a lot to learn about the game. Bird travels a path of excellence. The goal is not to reach an end point of perfection; he is living life in a way that recognizes there is always more to learn.

In 1985 Larry Bird was interviewed about his scoring slump. He said then that he wasn't in a slump, he was shooting the same as always but a lot of the shots that he thought would go in, didn't. A few weeks later he was interviewed again about getting over the slump and hitting this hot streak. Typically, Bird said that he was still shooting the same, but that now some shots he didn't think would go in, did. Bird refused to let thoughts get in his way. Thus he maintains his inner confidence even in the face of poor results, and he continues to develop his proficiency although he is already seen as the best. He is a professional.

A young woman decided to go to work as a waitress even though she knew nothing about the job except as a customer. Since she was told only how to write up tickets, place orders and carry trays, she realized that if she wanted to succeed, she would have to teach herself the rest of it. The first thing she began to notice was that customers want to be acknowledged but not pushed. So she paid attention to when people finished reading menus and were ready to order. Then she discovered that customers often ask for advice about the specials. So she made it her business to talk with the cooks before she started her shift, and to taste the dishes so she could advise her customers.

Next she observed that people don't like it when their food arrives either cold or dried out from sitting under the heat lamps. So she took some of her own time to hang around and familiarize herself with the system in the kitchen, and soon learned to estimate when her order would be ready. How to deal with different personalities, when to come back to check on things, making sure cups and glasses were refilled -- there was never an end to the things she learned about. The upshot was that her tips began to increase and customers began to request seating in her section. She had become a professional.

This direction of constantly improving goes hand in hand with involvement. With your eye on the lookout for better ways to serve customers, you can never be bored. Your level of involvement and presence is high, and your enjoyment of your work continues to grow. Everybody wins.

8

Don't Take It To Heart

With understanding, serving difficult people is simple.

Let's review some of the ground we've been covering. Understanding comes from knowing the way people function. Everyone has their unique world of thought that creates their unique experience of life which they see as their reality. What thoughts you are able to access at any given moment depends on your state of mind. So it makes perfect sense to each of us to do what we do at any moment, given our state of mind (level of understanding) and our unique thought system.

If your gentle dog has a bad bruise and you accidentally touch it when he isn't expecting it, you may get nipped. It's not a personal attack but rather an automatic reaction that the dog cannot control. When a customer barks at you it amounts to about the same thing. It is an automatic reaction, given the way that customer sees things at that moment.

An attack by another person isn't really directed at you personally.

I'll grant you that it often looks that way. People point fingers, make accusations, bring up history and supporting evidence, use your name -- and your ego tends to take all of this personally. But it really isn't directed at you. Your ego is nothing more than your self-image -- a part of your thought system. It is your thoughts about yourself in life. It is the way you see yourself and your surroundings via your particular thoughts. The job of your ego is to protect you and make sure you are always, always right.

This means, that what is coming in to you via sight, sound, and touch must be consistent with your existing thought system. Your ego does this by taking any untoward circumstance as a personal threat. Feelings of insecurity harden the ego's defensive shell.

In contrast to the hard-edged, empty manner created by the ego, there is a warm human rapport naturally generated within us. When we learn to tune out the static of ego, we are naturally left with the melody of deep human feelings -- unconditional love and compassion.

These deep human feelings of compassion and understanding -- which can only be released when you maintain your perspective -- melt away that defensive ego shell. It is seeing things not at the level of personality but at the level of humanity. It means responding from your innate well-being instead of letting others trigger your actions. You'll like the feeling of this because you are in control.

The better you feel about yourself, the less likely you are to lose your perspective, because at that higher state of mind you know how your thinking works. Feeling better about yourself requires nothing more than getting back in touch with the natural good feelings you were born with. The feelings are still there, but most of us tend to lose track of them and look outside ourselves to gauge how we're doing. We listen to what people think of us, look at our accomplishments, our status in society, to decide whether we are OK. At some point in our childhood we start to attach outer conditions to our well being. "I would be happy ...

> if Mom and Dad would love me more."
> if I had more money."
> if I could live in a certain house."
> if I could drive a particular car."
> if I could be successful at....."
> if others would only do what I want."
> if I were better looking" etc. etc. etc.

These conditions are the cause of dissatisfaction and unhappiness. The more a person strives to find peace of mind outside, the more a person learns it isn't there. As some philosopher once said, "You can never get enough of what you don't really want."

Quieting down and dropping those thoughts begins to put you back in touch with the deeper feelings. As these deeper feelings bubble up like a fresh, natural spring you feel better, your state of mind becomes more positive and, of course, life looks entirely different. Self-esteem is just allowing those innate good feelings to surface, which happens naturally when you drop negative thoughts.

The better the feeling you have, the more you understand how thinking works and the more compassion you have for your fellows. At these higher levels of understanding you see things in a wiser way. That doesn't mean cold and uncaring -- quite the opposite. It means that you do not take people's negativity as a personal matter. You see it for what it is: human frailty driven by insecurity.

It's not hard to serve nice people. It's the not-so-nice ones that present the challenge. Let's take a closer look at some common varieties of that Grade A distraction, the so-called difficult customer....

9

The Angry Customer

He walks through the door bellowing like a wounded bull. He is ready to attack anyone in sight, especially anyone who works for this business. You can tell that 'complain' is far too mild a word to describe what's about to happen. He's on the war path. Other angry customers may not be so flamboyant in their behavior, but they let you know they're angry.

Angry customers want to put you on the defensive. That's a normal protective reaction. If you oblige them you'll notice things get worse -- and that you have lost control. The customer will yell louder, may demand to see the boss, grow more abusive. And of course, you will become more defensive -- clam up, resort to tears, get angry yourself, and so on.

Anger is a by-product of fear. When you drive down the highway and someone cuts in on you, your first reaction is fear, quickly replaced by anger. "I'll show him!" If your mate or child is long overdue, you probably become anxious. The moment they walk through the door, instead of expressing relief, you probably show irritation or anger. "How

CUSTOMER SATISFACTION GUARANTEED

could you be so inconsiderate? You knew how worried I'd be."

When the angry customer walks in, the trick is to look beyond the angry behavior and realize you are witnessing a low state of mind, not a personal attack. These customers would be angry at anyone they met right now. Their upsets may not even have anything to do with your business or service. They are doubtless feeling frustrated and misunderstood. Even if something you have done or not done triggered their anger, it is still not really directed at you. Recognizing this fact is the first step in controlling your own reactions and starting to deal effectively with the customer. Instead of leading with your defenses, lead with your ear.

It's time to LISTEN. It's not enough to just hear the words, you must really listen so you <u>truly understand</u> the person. Since you know he has a unique view of things — that his anger is a result of his own state of mind lowered by negative thoughts — you know the solution is for him to start feeling lighter. By keeping your own good feeling and listening with compassion, you begin to defuse his anger. You can't fake it. If you are patronizing, if you listen from a superior, ego-driven position, the upset customer will grow even more angry.

Here is a scenario played out by two different bank tellers with the same customer. Notice the difference in tone.

A	**B**
<u>Customer</u>: *You people can't seem to get anything right. I've phoned four times to get this service charge dismissed, and it's still on my statement.*	<u>Customer</u>: *You people can't seem to get anything right. I've phoned four times to get this service charge dismissed and it's still on my statement.*

74

Teller A: I'm sorry, I don't know anything about it. That's not my department.
Customer: Now don't give me that stuff. All you people do is pass the buck. I'm sick of it. If you don't take care of it right now, I'm going to move my account to another bank.
Teller A: Well of course that's your prerogative, ma'm, but I don't think that is really necessary.
Customer: Then fix it! You're not supposed to charge me for checks.
Teller A: Yes, we do. We changed the policy a long time ago. You were notified by mail.
Customer: I most certainly was not. Besides, Mr. Jason told me when I opened my account that my checks would always be free. This is not right. I'm going straight to Mr. Jason and get this straightened out. And I'm going to talk to him about your attitude as well.
Teller A: You do what you have to do.

Teller B: Oh, I'm sorry you've had so much trouble. I'll see what I can do about it. Tell me what happened.
Customer (edge already off the anger): Well, I keep getting this charge for new checks. I was told in the beginning by Mr. Jason himself that there would be no charge for new checks. It's just not right.
Teller B: When did you open the account? 1980? Oh yes, back then we always offered free checks. Six months ago, the bank found that the cost of printing had gotten so high that we had to start charging for custom checks. We tried to tell all our customers about it. Perhaps the notice that came with your statement got misplaced.
Customer : Nobody told me about it. It's just not fair. Maybe I should move to another bank.
Teller B: I hope you won't do that. We want your business. Tell you what, I'll ask Mr. Jason if there's any way he can get the charges

removed this time, since you didn't know. Then the next time you order checks you'll know to expect the charge. Does that seem fair?

In the left-hand scenario you can see the customer's anger increasing. The reason is pretty obvious. The teller is not really listening, the teller is defending the banks position — being right. When people feel they're not being listened to, they try to get across harder and louder. The scenario on the right has a more understanding teller. Where Teller A displayed insecurity and defensiveness, Teller B showed understanding and warm feelings for this upset customer. The customer begins to feel more and more understood. She and the teller are now on the same team trying to resolve the problem instead of blaming each other. They reached a meeting of the minds.

You can tell if you are really listening to get an understanding with your customer by the way you feel. The deeper the understanding, the warmer the feeling. A bond of closeness develops between the two of you.

But what about the person who is full of negative feeling for no reason at all ....

10

The Disgruntled Ones

Unlike the angry customers, the nasty ones need no cause for negative behavior. You might think they had nails in their shoes or a panty girdle three sizes too small. These customers are absolutely not discriminating in their choice of targets for their negative feelings and biting language. They flunked out of diplomat school the first day.

It is perilously easy to react defensively to these people, and the more insecure you are the more likely you are to do so. The "nasty" provides the perfect opportunity to practice your skill at relieving the pressure.

When you see one of these people walk through the door, you want to remind yourself that the poor soul is living in hell. Truly. I know they act as if they are out to get you, but look at it this way: would you or anyone you know want to live in a world where everything is negative? In order for someone to act this way they must actually see things that way. Their boorish manner is not just an act they put on when they walk into your business. This is the life they live inside themselves. Their state of mind is so negative that they must lash out at the whole world.

It's time to apply the helium principle.

The only way to deal with these people is with all the compassion and warm human feeling you can muster. It's easier when you realize the terrible life they must live. They're just like people suffering under a severe physical handicap that your heart goes out to. The nasties have a severe handicap too -- the thoughts in their heads! Just a little understanding and warm feeling goes a long way. You may not change them but you can keep from making things worse for them. More importantly, you can protect yourself from getting dragged down into their mood.

Focus on serving the needs of the nasty. The more in-service feeling you can muster the more effective you will be. To be in service, you must go beyond your personal needs and ego, focus on something bigger than yourself. Whenever you feel yourself slipping into negative reactions, placing yourself in a service state of mind is a sure start to more positive feelings and greater ease in dealing with people.

To see how this works, consider an example. In a restaurant one night, the waitress threw the menus at my wife and me, snapped that she would be back, and stomped away. She projected so much negative feeling that we looked at each other and considered walking out. But the place has the best pizza in town. The waitress finally returned with a surly "Whatdayawant," and I started to bristle. Then, all of a sudden, I got past my own ego and realized what was going on. She was feeling rushed and worn out. I've been there too, so with a genuine warm feeling of understanding I said, "Looks like you're having a hard night." She looked up from her order book and her whole body relaxed. She half smiled and confessed, "I sure am. We're really busy, and one of the girls didn't show up."

The warm feeling that passed between us lifted her spirits and her whole attitude became noticeably more pleasant. Not only did she serve us well, but she was, we noticed, friendlier to her other customers as well.

I am continually astonished by the power of genuine human feelings. A few seconds of compassion will do more to change people than hours of talk.

Now how about the customer who has a nice feeling but doesn't want to talk ....

- Habits are like a suit of armor that people step into when they feel insecure. The armored person's actions follow the laws of habit and not the laws of common sense.

- Compasion and understanding help other people move out of insecurity and habits.

11

The Non-Communicator

She walks in to try on some clothes. You ask if you can help, but you don't hear any reply so you step back and wait. She looks around and then sorts through some racks. After a few minutes she looks a little lost, so you again ask if you can be of assistance. This time she replies, but you don't really understand what she is saying. She seems to mumble and speak so softly that you're never really sure what she says. When you show her a dress, you can't tell whether she likes it or doesn't. "Uh huh" and "OK" doesn't tell much about what she's thinking. You wonder if she's wired for sound.

This customer is challenging in a quite different way. We are used to measuring other people's range of response in relation to our own. Since you deal with the public regularly, you probably have a fairly wide range of response and are somewhat outgoing in nature. The clam lives in a different reality. She has a range but it is much more subtle. If she is ecstatic about something she may come up with "It's OK." If she's turned off you may hear, "I'm not sure."

It's important not to fall into judgment of the clams because chances are they are quite sensitive to feelings. This is your key to serving them well. Don't focus on the content of words, but on the feeling behind the words. If she is shy and insecure, your warm understanding will make it easier for her to tell you what's on her mind. As you observe and listen carefully you will soon catch on to her range of response.

This is a wonderful opportunity to see the world through another set of glasses. By tuning in at the feeling level you will be able to moderate your own responses so this kind of customer will be more comfortable with you. Someone who is quiet and soft spoken may be turned off by exuberance, but by focusing on the feeling connection, you will instinctively respond in the most appropriate manner. A warm "Feel free to browse and let me know when I can be of service" may be all that's needed.

But what about those who are the opposite -- pushy....

12
—

The Demanding Client

This guy walks through the door and takes over. He'd make a splendid Marine drill instructor. He demands. His standards for your performance are always higher than you can deliver. He has strong opinions about everyone and everything in your business. He knows you were set on earth for no other purpose but to do or die at his bidding. He is a grade A pain in the neck. And he has plenty of female counterparts.

Most of us react to the drillmaster with rigidity and stubbornness. Somehow a bossy person raises our hackles. I don't suppose many of us enjoy being treated like lackeys, and most of us tend to take it as a personal affront.

The demanding customer needs to feel in control of everything around him. It gives him a sense of power and self-importance that quiets his own insecurities. His opinions are rigid because he does not understand that they are just his thoughts. For him this is how it is. Threatened, he becomes even bossier -- if you can imagine that.

Ignore his opinions. Like the rest of us, he has his own set. Treat him with the respect due every human being, but don't kowtow. Respond to his needs but not his manner. Here are two sample dialogues. The left-hand column shows a waitress who reacts to a bossy customer; the right-hand column, a waitress who is able to penetrate his disguise. The words are not the point; it's where the tone leads. To ill will on the left, a relaxed customer on the right.

<u>W.</u> Good evening, sir, let me tell you about the specials.
<u>C.</u> Don't bother, I know exactly what I want and it's not on the menu. First, warm bread, and butter that is not frozen in little cubes you can't spread. Second, tenderloin steak cooked medium rare -- a hint of pink only. Third, baked potato with sour cream and chives -- and I don't want any onion tops, or dried substitute; authentic, fresh chopped chives. Fourth, green peas not

<u>W.</u> Good evening, sir. May I tell you about the specials?
<u>C.</u> Don't bother, I know exactly what I want and it's not on the menu. First, warm bread, and butter that is not frozen in little cubes you can't spread. Second, tenderloin steak cooked medium rare -- a hint of pink only. Third, baked potato with sour cream and chives -- and I don't want any onion tops, or dried substitute; authentic, fresh chopped chives. Fourth, green peas not

over cooked -- they must be firm, and a Caesar.....

_W._ (bristling) Excuse me sir, but we don't offer a custom menu. The chef fixes the menu and that's all we can offer. Why don't your try the....

_C._ Maybe I didn't make myself clear. I am the customer here. Your job is to take care of me. Is that understood? Because if it isn't, then let's get the manager right now.

_W._ (becoming submissive, yet resentful). OK, OK, let's not make a federal case out of this. What am I supposed to do if the chef won't cook what you want?

_C._ What you're supposed to do is your job -- and that is to take my order and bring me my food the way I want it.

_W._ Yes sir. If you want steak, sir, it will have to be filet since we don't have tenderloin. The vegetable tonight is green over cooked -- they must be firm, and a Caesar salad. And make sure you rub the bowl with garlic and mash the anchovies.

_W._ (amused) You certainly are a man who knows exactly what he wants. That must make things a lot simpler in your life.

_C._ (interested) What do you mean, simpler?

_W._ Well, you don't have to waste time making up your mind or agonizing over decisions. I mean tonight,for example, you might have trouble deciding between the tourenados of beef with Bearnaise sauce and the Greek filet which is a 7-ounce filet filled with feta cheese, mesquite grilled to perfection.

_C._ To tell you the truth I always order the same thing because I've been disappointed so often. At least I know when I get my steak and baked potato it will be the same.

*beans. And we offer a din-
ner or spinach salad....*
*C. You know you have an
attitude problem. I won't
stand for your surly man-
ner.*
*W. (Huffing off) I don't have
to put up with this.*

*W. We don't have exactly
what you want to order, but
I can come as close as possible or, if you'll allow me to
suggest an alternative, you
might be pleasantly
surprised with something a
little out of the ordinary.*
*C. I'll listen but I'll tell you
right now if I don't like it I
won't pay for it.*
*W. Having you leave here a
satisfied customer is my
primary concern. Now lis-
ten to this. How does ......*

Demands are nothing more than needs dressed up to
look like rights. If you can see through the disguise, you
may find a decent person underneath the dictator pretense.

Again, it is the true human feeling that does the work.
You can't pretend. If you try, you'll come across as obse-
quious (which will only make him worse). It helps to realize
that this customer finds it a tiring burden to run the whole
world. Your deeper understanding is actually a relief to the
drillmaster. If you give him a chance to relax by letting him
know you care about him but will not be browbeaten, he
will feel more comfortable, less driven by his need to be in
control of the whole world lest it take advantage of him.

Then there are the compulsive talkers ....

13
—

The Endless Talker

When you ask her for her boarding pass with seat assignment, motormouth starts in on the story of her life. When you ask her to buckle her seat belt she wants to discuss moving to a seat next to that passenger -- no, perhaps the one over there, who looks more.... Selecting the main course is the signal for a long dissertation that wanders from food to parties to.... Every time you pass by she wants to hold on and talk for dear life.

Service people tend to either ignore or indulge motormouth. Neither response works. Like a hungry cat, you'll find her tripping you up very time you turn around.

If you indulge her she will never get enough. She'll hog your time while the other customers fume. She is lonely and insecure. All of her talk is to fill an empty feeling inside -- a need for human contact.

Bring the endless talker maximum presence and minimum conversation. Presence is super-concentrated attention. Like a rich dessert, a small amount can fill up even a greedy person. I remember my children, when they were small, would tug at my trousers, make noise, jabber away, anything to get my attention when I was busy with something else. If I told them to go away, they would be right back at it in less than five minutes. Finally, I began to realize that what they wanted at those moments is presence.

Let's take the situation in the airplane and construct a dialogue to show how concentrated presence might work.

Passenger (P): Excuse me, miss, but could you tell me what we're flying over now?
Flight attendant (FA): Certainly. Let's see, I'd say somewhere over Nebraska.
P: Oh, I have an uncle who lives in Nebraska. Have you ever been to Nebraska.
FA: (about to leave) No, can't say that I have. Well, if you'll excuse me....
P: (trying to hold on) Are those portable phones very expensive? I thought I might call my uncle if we're somewhere near his house.
FA: (recognizing what's really going on) They're a lot more expensive than calling from the ground. (dropping all other distractions for the moment) It sounds to me like you really like your family and enjoy being around people. It's not easy traveling alone, is it? (a warm feeling of understanding rises) Tell you what. I have a lot to do

*for the first part of this trip --
meals to prepare and serve,
that sort of thing. But later on I'll
have some time. Maybe we can
talk then if you feel like it. I'd like
to hear more about your family.
OK?*
*P: (feeling more secure and
relaxed) Oh that would be nice.
You go ahead with your work.
(to the passenger next to her)
She's certainly nice, isn't she?*

The talker wants all of you, with nothing else on your mind. With my children, it turned out that thirty seconds of total presence contented them and away they went. It's your best bet in dealing with the incessant talker.

How about when the talk turns personal ....

- Habits and patterns will disappear when they are starved of insecurity and attention.

14

The Hustler

He walks up to your counter and starts admiring the display of women's accessories. "I'm looking for something unusual for a very special person." The next thing you know this smoothie is more interested in what you might have to offer than what the store sells. He may well be a legitimate customer, but his dialogue has become very personal. If you want to play his game, I don't need to tell you what to do.

Most customer service people either become embarrassed or harden up. Neither is helpful nor necessary to stop the nonsense without losing business.

Here is a customer who finds you attractive and wants to get to know you better. True, he has a specific idea about the form that should take. Although he may be trying to prove he is attractive (the old ego game), his underlying need is for closer human contact. In his own way he is lonely and insecure. If you maintain your human warmth but stick to business, you'll find that you can ignore the second meanings of his words and glances and treat him like anyone else.

If you're forced to redirect his conversation, your warm understanding manner will protect him from feeling rebuffed. He may walk away thinking you must be stupid not to pick up on his real meaning, but he won't feel wounded.

Here are two dialogues between the sales person (SP) and the hustling customer (HC). As before, don't pay attention to the words; this is not some technique. Notice the flow of the conversation and the resulting feeling. In the left-hand column the sales person goes into reaction. In the right-hand column the sales person keeps a nice feeling without getting hooked.

<u>HC:</u> *I'm looking for something sexy and intimate for a special friend. A slinky negligee, bikini briefs -- I'm not sure what.*
<u>SP:</u> *(feeling slight discomfort with his manner) There's a rack of women's intimate wear over there.*
<u>HC:</u> *(relishing her discomfort) I'm terrible at deciding these things. Could you come over and help me decide? She's built a lot like you.*

<u>HC:</u> *I'm looking for something sexy and intimate for a special friend. A slinky negligee, bikini briefs -- I'm not sure what.*
<u>SP:</u> *We have a wonderful selection of items. Let me show you some things and perhaps you'll get some ideas.*
<u>HC:</u> *(with a meaningful glance) I've already got a few. Why don't you show me what you've got.*

SP: Uh, sure. What did you have in mind?

HC: (gleam in his eye). Oh, plenty. Let's see, this little number looks fun. Would you mind holding it up so I can get an idea of how it might look?

SP: (becoming turned off and resistant) Look, my job doesn't require that I model. I'll give you my opinion -- period!

HC: You're even cuter when you're upset. I'll bet you're a real fighter. I like my women with plenty of fire.

SP: (feeling threatened) If you want to buy something, fine. Otherwise I'm going to wait on other customers.

HC: Tsk, tsk, don't get huffy, sweetheart. After all I am the customer here.

SP: (embarrassed and angry) I'd better get the manager, maybe she can take care of you. I certainly can't.

HC: Don't bother, I've lost interest.

SP: (ignoring the obvious) Here are some lovely nightgowns and over there, more intimate items.

HC: Yeah, intimate is what I like. Show me something that might turn me on.

SP: (warm and understanding manner) Most women like subtlety rather than brazen overstatement -- in most everything. So I suggest that you choose something that is more flattering to her than revealing.

HC: But I like the revealing stuff, that's what turns me on. What turns you on?

SP: (centered and in control) I've known a lot of men who thought that too, but most of the women I know aren't like that. What's your special friend like?

HC: She's a lot like you. Pretty, great build, nice eyes...

SP: (unperturbed) If she is anything like me, then I suggest you consider this luxurious night gown.

It has beautiful lace work that any woman would really appreciate. And you'll notice from the design and construction that it is flattering but not in bad taste.
HC: (losing his assurance but still trying) Could you maybe try it on so I can see what it would look like on her?
SP: (amused and chuckling) Let me guess. You are a comedian practicing your next routine; we're really on Candid Camera! No, I'm afraid you'll just have to imagine what this will look like on your special friend. If she doesn't like it, you can always return or exchange it. Would you like it gift wrapped?

So long as you maintain a warm, friendly manner and keep focused on serving the customer, even the hustler's act can't create problems. The power of pure human presence protects you and gives your customers permission to drop their act and become real.

Now how do you learn to get along with the egomaniac?....

15

The Obnoxious Personality

He is the best. He knows more, has done more, and is better than anyone at most anything. If you don't believe it, just ask him. This is the original Ugly American. Everything is designed to impress. Although he may not know what he's talking about, he says it with arrogance to make everyone think he is the expert.

"Waiter bring me a carafe of your house white. What year is it? What, your house wine isn't vintage?" "I want 'zorbay' after my hamburger to clear my palate." He snaps his fingers and talks down to everyone in the restaurant. Those who are unfortunate enough to be sitting nearby are forced to listen to his disdainful remarks -- and may even be corralled into his conversations.

What's beneath that inflated ego is an empty cavity. The bigger the ego, the greater the underlying insecurity. Service people usually wince and become indignant -- which is fuel for his fire.

Ignore his manner and treat him as you would anyone else. If he sees you are not a threat to his insecurity, and are not going to feed it by being impressed, you will soon see he is a pretty lonely fellow. When you meet his bluster with a genuine desire to help, his puffed chest will begin to deflate. This is easy to do when you recognize what his behavior really signals.

If you felt as insecure and lonely as he, you might be acting the same way. In fact to some degree all of us behave this way when we are insecure. Did you ever try to impress someone with how much you know? Or notice yourself dressing in "power clothes" for an interview?

There is a slim, ordinary looking small ocean fish called a puffer. When threatened, he pumps himself up to a ball several times his normal size with thorns sticking out all over. Predators won't touch him because he looks quite intimidating, and quite indigestible.

When I run into an obnoxious egomaniac, this picture comes to mind and promptly puts things into perspective for me. I know that reducing his insecurity by letting him know my deeper feelings for him will take the air out of his balloon and allow him to operate like the ordinary human being he really is.

Let's take the waiter in the situation above and see how he might handle this customer. This time we'll just go through a dialogue that leads to a satisfactory handling of the customer. As always, it is not the words but the state of mind the waiter maintains that is important, the sentiment behind the words.

> _C._ Waiter! Waiter! My dear boy, can't you see that I'm waiting. I want a carafe of your finest house wine. What brand is it? Is it a vintage year?
> _W._ Sorry to keep you waiting but I wanted to be sure the food for the next table was delivered

while it was hot. Our house wines are excellent -- small winery up-state. You might not have heard of it but I'm sure you'll enjoy their wine.

C. Very well, I'll try the white but if I don't like it I'm not going to pay for it. You know the quality of the wine depends on the acidity and drainage of the soil, the temperature during the growing season and so many factors. Very few vineyards are able to produce a truly great wine in this part of the country.

W. Well, I'm reasonably sure you'll enjoy it. Now let me tell you about the specials tonight. We have a red snapper, mesquite broiled, with a light lemon-butter, tarragon sauce that is light and delicious.

C. Is the tarragon fresh and crushed by hand? Because if you don't crush by hand you can bruise it and impair the full flavor.

W. (undaunted) Our chef has gained quite a reputation for his fine cuisine. He never shares the details of his recipes but I can attest to the results. I tasted the red snapper tonight and it's wonderful.

C. I presume that you serve sor-

bet between courses to cleanse the palate. If you don't do that you contaminate one dish with another.

W. (with fond feelings) We used to but when Enrique came he stopped it. He says that a fine chef takes all those factors into account in preparing the meal. That's why our meals come as a totally designed dinner from soup to dessert. Each selection is blended to complement the flavor of the other.

C. (with a trace of humility) My, my. That's something I have never heard of before. Perhaps this will be an excellent dinner after all. Yes, I'll try the red snapper -- with extra fresh lemon on the side, of course.

W. (delighted that this 'difficult' customer turns out to be human) But of course. You've made a good choice. I know you'll really like it. To go with the red snapper, may I recommend a slightly different wine for your consideration?...

Clearly, every situation is different so there is no pat approach or dialogue you can use. Meeting your customer with fond feelings and deep understanding allows your customer to relax and be more natural -- and keeps you enjoying your job.

Yes, you say but sometimes we get some real
wierdos ....

- Respect is the door to human connectedness, deeper feelings, and growing appreciation in any relationship. Without this respect friction and resentment result.

16

The Eccentric

He looks a bit like a retired British officer. As you see him sitting alone at dinner he appears to be in deep conversation with the empty chair across from him.

Here she comes again. Her flamboyant clothes and picture hat aren't so bad, although they are from another era; it's her tendency to bring out old publicity photos and offer autographs to your clients that concerns you. Still, some people find her refreshing.

Welcome to the wacky world of eccentric characters. It's really easy for you to become self-conscious, and to be embarrassed by the behavior of these customers. Just because they are "different," you may feel uncomfortable. Sometimes I get the feeling people are afraid that if they get too close to these characters they will catch the weirdness.

You know they are harmless and probably lonely, that their behavior is only an attempt to fill their need to be noticed. In fact all the eccentrics I have run into have turned out to be quite lonely, but the very mannerisms they use to get attention end up driving people away.

As we discussed earlier, this is an example of a person's thought system creating reality, even if it appears unsatisfactory. Eccentrics, seeing themselves as not fitting in, dress and act in a way that does not fit the norm, and then experience not being accepted.

Even eccentrics have the right to be treated as customers. When you see that they are just a more obvious example of the uniqueness of everyone's own culture -- a thought system that is like nobody else's -- you will feel more comfortable dealing with them.

If their mannerisms are disturbing others, you can often solve the problem by soliciting the eccentric's aid in protecting other people's rights. Something as simple as "I know you are generous about sharing your memories with others, but some people really treasure their privacy; you can understand that can't you?" will make an ally for you. When they feel your acceptance, a warm rapport may spring up between you that allows them to modify their eccentric behavior. Look upon them as colorful accents in a too-often humdrum world.

Recently I talked with an elderly lady whose relatives told me she behaved very strangely. What I found was an old lady who had great difficulty remembering recent events. She could recall what had happened five, ten, or twenty years ago, but her short-term memory was gone. Her "strange" behavior was simply the result of not being able to remember what happened and had been said five minutes ago or yesterday.

Her behavior (or perhaps their fears that the same thing might happen to them someday) frightened the family. She sensed the difference in them and began to feel insecure herself. I found that if I ignored her mannerisms and patiently re-answered her repeating questions, we were able to have a pleasant and sensible chat. Her normally anxious and irritable manner gave way to her natural good feelings.

As she felt more secure she actually began to remember a bit better; that is, she acted more "normal."

Then there is the customer who can never seems to make up her mind....

- Compatibility of personality, interests, and desires is a weak basis for a relationship. The deep feelings of gratitude for being together is an enduring basis.

17

The Undecided

She has already looked at fifteen pairs of shoes and none of them seems just right. She appears serious about buying, but just can't make up her mind. The more you suggest, the more confused she seems to get. If it weren't for the fact that you have four other customers waiting, you might be willing to stick with her all afternoon -- which is how long she seems to need.

Service people normally grow impatient with the customers who have trouble making up their minds. The normal reaction is to pressure or abandon them. Either course turns them into unhappy customers.

To understand this kind of person we must go back to the discussion of thought systems. Those who can't make up their minds are those who are terrified of making a wrong decision. They do not trust themselves. They are afraid someone won't like it or that they might get home and find it "just isn't right." To another person it might be nothing, but to the indecisive, this is a big decision with far reaching impact. Another woman might easily take any pair, prepared to exchange them later if she decided they didn't suit her.

Indecision is fired by -- you guessed it -- insecurity. So, of course, the first thing you can do is to create a calm, reassuring environment. This means putting no pressure on her to make a decision, so you certainly don't want to hover. "Take your time. I know how difficult it is sometimes to find just the right pair. Let me know when I can help." Your understanding manner will bolster this customer's confidence in herself.

Don't take doubt seriously. It's something everyone goes through. When she works through it, she won't need any input from you.

If she does ask for help, remember that feeling overwhelmed adds to insecurity, so try to help this customer limit the possibilities. When I sold shoes years ago, the rule was to show customers only two pair of shoes at a time so they would find it easier to decide.

I've often watched savvy sales people in restaurants and clothing stores offer authentic suggestions to help customers narrow the field of choice. When possible, you can help by giving customers a way out, by offering an option to return or exchange their purchase if they don't like it when they get it home. It's the threat of having to make the final choice that really bothers this kind of customer. After all, they are going to have to live with it. Patience and understanding will make it much easier for them to reach a decision.

If you have to leave them to take care of other customers, take care not to make the dithered customer wrong for not having decided. The waitress who huffs off because you can't choose quickly has a hard time re-establishing rapport with the customer.

Then there's the cheapskate....

18

The Skimpy Tipper

Here she comes again. She gets a styling, perm, facial, manicure and pedicure. She's very fussy about having everything done just so, and even asks you to correct imaginary little flaws. Her bill is seldom less than $100. With flourish she tips you a whole dollar -- and expects you to share it with the manicurist. Wow!

When they recognize her, many service people either pour on phony extra service or skimp their service to her. Neither of these tactics will change her. Remember that each of us has our unique world view. Each of us has certain vanities, values and beliefs based on the experiences which we have collected over our lifetime. The skimpy tipper believes she is doing the appropriate thing. Her logic dictates her actions.

There are still people who went through the great depression when money was scarce and people were hungry. Some of them to this day maintain a several month's supply of canned goods -- just in case. There are people alive today who still don't trust their money to banks because they lost everything in '29. Circumstances change, but our beliefs and habits often lag behind.

There is a classic behavioral study of a voracious game fish called pike. Scientists placed a pike in a tank with a dozen minnows which promptly disappeared. Next they isolated the pike in a clear glass cylinder within the tank so the pike couldn't reach the minnows. For the first few hours the pike darted for the minnows, smashing its snout against the invisible barrier. On the second day, the pike quit trying; it had learned that chasing minnows meant a bump on the snout not a meal. When they removed the glass divider the pike continued to ignore the minnows and eventually starved to death, so strong was the conditioning.

We are certainly smarter than fish but our habits and assumptions dictate a surprising amount of our daily behavior.

If you pour extra attention and service on the tightwad, she might appreciate it, but she's more likely to suspect your motives. If you treat her shabbily, she will resent it, and you will have to suffer your own shabby feeling. The answer is to treat this customer like any other. Her business is important and helps pay the bills. If she feels well served she is likely to recommend you and your business to others. It helps you if you remind yourself that in the grand scheme of things, her low tips will be balanced by the more generous ones.

It's been interesting for me to see my own limitations in the area of tips. For most of my life I resented tipping because I felt that service was part of the job service people were paid for. Later I learned that many service people are paid minimum wage in the expectation tips will make up the difference. Thus tips are, in fact, a vital part of their income.

The resentment disappeared but my 10% guideline remained. I didn't approve of the system, but I couldn't penalize the individuals who served me for it. Not until one of my sons worked as a hotel valet and doorman did I come to fully understand how it really is. Since then I gladly tip well.

Adults are one thing, but what about the little monsters....

- Communication is a hollow conduit that has no inherent power to help or hurt a relationship. The feeling state that travels through the conduit is the power that impacts relationships.

19

The Unruly Child

They are sweet little angels -- their dad said so. But in your waiting room they are waging war. Other customers are watching warily to duck the next flying object. If the brats are not throwing something, or yelling, they're racing around playing hide-and-seek between the chairs.

You may blame the parent and resent the fact that he is not controlling his children, but this only threatens his self-esteem. You can be sure he is already feeling a little uncomfortable and perhaps downright embarrassed at his offspring's rowdy behavior. Any negative feelings you contribute will only make matters worse.

Patience and quiet are seldom part of the life of these youngsters. They have tremendous energy that reaches a critical mass and explodes when there are two or more in the same room. If you try a heavy-handed approach to make them behave, you may succeed temporarily but you'll create more problems than you solve.

It is much easier to divert their energy than to suppress it. Offer them toys, books, simple games to occupy their attention. Some restaurants automatically bring coloring books and crayons to kids. I've visited doctors' and dentists' offices, grocery stores, and drive-in movies with special corners fenced off and furnished with dolls, Tonka trucks and games for the little rascals. One haircutting franchise shows cartoons -- and the kids want to come back often.

The only children around our house now are visiting grandchildren, but we have a laundry basket stuffed with dolls, games, coloring books, Legos, little cars, etc, and the kids make a beeline for it as soon as they arrive. Such a basket might solve some problems in your place of business.

And don't worry about other customers' reactions. Most people understand that kids will be kids. We were all that size once. In fact I've seen adults sitting in a waiting room jump in to help entertain the kids, while to others the kids are entertainment.

Now to a better understanding of people who seem critical most of the time ....

20

The Critic

The front desk phone rings. It's the busiest check-in time, with people waiting three deep for their room assignments. Of course! It's the complainer in room 326 again. The last time she called, the carpeting didn't look freshly vacuumed. She complained to the bellman that you don't supply free shampoo like the hotel down the street. (Why didn't she go there?). And housekeeping already reported that she wants the blankets replaced because they look used. Now she wants to know if you have a room with a better view!

You probably feel lacking when you deal with the critic. You may get defensive and indignant, or patronizing. Neither works because they both aggravate the insecurity of these customers and inflame their need for attention. When the critics show up at those moments when you are feeling overwhelmed by more justifiable demands, you may fume with resentment. Beware! Your negativity will communicate itself to the customer regardless of your words and will most likely escalate the cycle for attention.

Some critics are critical out of sheer habit. Somewhere along the line they learned that if they find enough fault with the world around them they get to feel superior. Others grew up copying the pattern from a parent. Each of them becomes more critical as he or she feels more insecure. Just remember that all habitual negative thinking and behavior is driven by insecurity.

You cannot ignore the critic, nor can you give in to every demand. The best approach is to overlook their critical behavior and respond to the real need as best you can. If you bring the customer high presence at least they will get the nice feeling of being understood and appreciated. If you cannot meet their demands, explain why without belittling their criticism.

Here are two scenarios dealing with a critic; the left hand column leaves a bitter taste, the right hand leads to a meeting of the minds.

Guest: This is Mrs. Simpson in 326. I don't like the view. I want to look at something better than the parking lot.

Clerk: (rushed and irritated) I'm sorry Mrs. Simpson but that is the best we can do.

Guest: (getting more upset) I don't like your attitude, young man. When I stay in a hotel this expensive I expect to be treated well.

Guest: This is Mrs. Simpson in 326. I don't like the view. I want to look at something better than the parking lot.

Clerk: Yes, Mrs. Simpson, what seems to be the problem?

Cust: Well it just seems to me that I deserve a room with a view of something better than this.

Clerk: Most of the rooms have the same view except for the

Clerk: (resentful) Look, ma'm, I'm doing the best I can. You called at the busiest time. We have ten people waiting to check in and I really don't have time to handle this right now.

Guest: Are you going to do something about it or do I have to contact the manager?

Clerk: Look if you want to call back in an hour I'll see what we can do about another room but I doubt there is anything else. We're busy.

Guest: Somebody's going to hear plenty about this. (slams phone down)

few that look out on the pool area. But of course those might not be as quiet for you.

Guest: I'd like to examine one of those to see if they are any better.

Clerk: (calm, understanding) Right at this moment we have a large group of people waiting to check in, Mrs. Simpson. I'll be glad to see what is available and call you back in a little while when I can properly take care of you. Is that OK?

Guest:(still persists) By then won't all of those rooms be gone?

Clerk: Of course if anyone reserved one of those rooms we have to give it to them. But I promise I'll save one for you if any are available. I'll call you back in about thirty minutes.

In their own way the critics are just trying to make sure they get what seems to them their due. For every such nuisance there are many more customers who do you a favor by letting you know what does in fact need to be corrected. It's all part of the feedback that keeps your business on track.

What do you do with a loaded customer?..

- Emotions can be understood only as a phenomenon. They do not lend themselves to analysis with regard to cause or intensity. Consequently, the healthiest stance towards negative emotions is disrespect and disregard.

21

The Intoxicated Guest

People come to your establishment to drink, to unwind from a hard day, to forget, perhaps to find companionship. You expect a certain amount of noise and a loosening of behavior. But there is a limit. When she decides to debut as an opera singer, or he fancies himself Don Juan or worse, turns into the evil side of his jekyll-and-hyde personality, then they've gone the limit.

Other patrons will probably find the drunk's behavior amusing or at least predictable in an establishment that serves liquor. You may find their behavior less than amusing, perhaps unnerving, and even dangerous. Service people are usually more worried and concerned than the other patrons. Customers can leave whenever they want. Getting tough with the inebriated customer can backfire; ignoring him may be taken as condoning the behavior.

People drink to relax, to get away from their daily problems and pressures, to escape their headful of thoughts. They drink to feel better. Whatever action you take, do it with understanding.

If you react with negative feeling you'll only make matters worse. Even customers who are annoyed by the behavior may feel you've been too rough if you don't handle the situation with tact. (After all, they may be the one to create the problem the next time.)

Most establishments that serve alcohol have policies and procedures for handling the customer who has had too much. In many states the law holds the establishment liable for an accident involving a drunk driver who was served too many drinks. Stop serving when common sense tells you the customer has had enough.

What you do is not as important as the feeling behind it. The bizarre behavior of most people can be handled gracefully by treating people firmly but with nice feeling. The human feeling helps to keep people from reacting badly, and the firmness penetrates their fuzzy heads.

Sometimes drunks take refusal as an insult and many get fighting mad about it even if they were not belligerent before. A successful bouncer will have the physical build to represent the firmness and a gentle manner to soothe the customer's reactions. Buddy Baer, the seven-foot, three hundred pound brother of Max Baer the heavy-weight boxer, owned a bar. One night an intoxicated customer grew belligerent and started making a nuisance of himself. Buddy walked up behind the man and gently placed his mitt-sized hand on the hothead's shoulder. The man glanced at the hand, then gazed up two feet into the friendly face of this Herculean giant. Without a peep, he left the bar.

One of my daughters had a part time job as a waitress at a night club. I asked her if she was bothered often by drunks, and how she handled it. "Almost every night at least one customer gets too much to drink and decides he is the original lover boy. He'll tell me he's madly in love with me and wants to take me home. I laugh and tell him to wait and see how he feels when he wakes up in the morning. I'm always nice to my customers, and they never give me any trouble."

Not taking things too personally, and keeping your good feelings toward people are powerful solutions to people problems.

But what do you do when customers <u>really</u> get loud?...

- To the extent that stress accompanies an action, the ease and ultimate value of that action is reduced accordingly. Any action would be more efficiently and effectively accomplished without stress.

22

The Fighter

As you approach this couple's table you can feel the hostility between them. They are steaming, and you wonder why they are even out together. It's no surprise to you when they erupt into a shouting match that stops conversation in the entire restaurant. And lucky you! You get to be the referee.

Customers and service people alike yearn to get as far as possible from these scenes. They're frightening, and we don't want to get involved in a quarrel that is not ours; we have our own problems.

People fight and argue out of a feeling of frustration and upset. The more they argue, the less they listen. The less people feel understood, the more upset and negative they become.

With warm human feeling blocked between these two, it makes perfect sense -- to them -- to be fighting. After all, everything looks rotten in their foul mood, particularly the behavior of the person seated across the table. Any outside threat will only add to their insecurities and bad feelings so a heavy-handed approach is definitely not in order here. You don't know their rules.

You may find that the squall blows over in short order, so letting the situation ride may be the best course as long as other customers don't fret. Any outside interference in their civil war could unite them instantly and turn the intruder into their common enemy.

If you do decide you should intervene, the key is to do so with maximum understanding. Your good feeling and compassion will tend to pull them into a better mood or at least not aggravate the situation. Ask for their cooperation in respecting the rights of other customers to enjoy a peaceful meal. Let's look at the feeling behind two possible dialogues: the one on the left leads to bigger trouble, while the one on the right leads towards a meeting of the minds.

Waiter: (uneasy) Excuse me folks but you'll have to keep the noise down. You're bothering other customers.
He: Mind your own business.
She: See, I told you you're a loud mouth.
He: I'm not talking to you so shut up. Look, mister, I'm already upset about your service so leave us alone.

Waiter: (gently) Hi. I'm terribly sorry to intrude in your private affairs, but other customers have started to complain about the noise. I would really appreciate it if you could lower your voices.
He: I don't think we're disturbing anyone else. Just leave us alone.
She: I told you we were getting too loud.

<u>Waiter:</u> *(voice raised)*
Look, I'm trying to be civil to you. You can't scream and yell like this. If you can't be decent, I'll have to ask you to leave.
<u>He:</u> *You bet! But I'm damned if I'll pay for the meal. It wasn't that good anyway.*
<u>Waiter:</u> *(becoming irate)*
Now just a minute, if you think ....

<u>Waiter:</u> *(full of compassion)*
Believe me I wouldn't say anything if I hadn't had complaints. If you need some privacy I'd be glad to arrange for you to use the manager's office.
<u>He:</u> *OK, OK. We'll take care of it.*
<u>Waiter:</u> *(sincere gratitude)*
Thank you, it sure makes my job easier. Can I get something for you?

Your conversation would depend entirely on the situation. You can see, however, that in the scenario on the right the ill feeling is subsiding because the sentiment behind the waiter's words is warm and understanding. In the left hand scenario, the waiter became insecure and defensive, fueling the fire.

While it is not your place to be a counselor, the following story may help your understanding while interacting with distressed couples.

A couple, worn out from arguing and fighting, came to us for help. When upset, she would scream and yell. He would then get upset with her "irrational" behavior and yell back. Then both would steam around in silence for hours, avoiding each other. Hours or days later, they would sheepishly kiss and make up. They had gone through this cycle several times a month for years. The moments of making up had become their only times of closeness.

They began to realize they fought because they had lost the nice feelings for each other; their thinking became distorted, which pulled down their state of mind. Once their mood got low enough, everything looked negative, which twisted their logic so they could not help lashing out at each other.

They started to understand that their negative behavior was simply the aftermath of a low state of mind, but by then it was already too late to correct the behavior. This insight made it easier for each of them to meet the negative feelings of the other with more compassion and understanding. They could see that the answer lay in finding the nice feelings again -- the arguments would handle themselves.

So if you run into a pair of fighters, remember the helium principle. Bringing a high level of deep human understanding is the best remedy for any negative situation.

Now let's talk about gloomy gus..........

23

The Depressed Person

He sits down in your chair for a haircut, but you're not sure you can even see his hair for the black cloud of doom and gloom that hangs heavy over his head. When you say good morning he growls, "If you say so." Although you know your job is to reshape his hair not his attitude, you know nothing you do will look good through his depressed filters. What to do?

Nothing. The last thing you want to do in this situation is worry about his gloomy mood. People get into low moods as a result of their negative thoughts. As they worry about and analyze "the problem," their mood-tide ebbs. The more negative the situation looks, the lower their state of mind, and the more negative the outlook. This downward spiral can start with the simplest thought.

Suppose you had the wonderful impulse to follow a whim and fly to Hawaii for a week. It's something you've always wanted to do and your best friend would probably go along. The thought thrills you, your mood soars. The next moment you start to consider the practicalities. Beware! How much do tickets cost? Do you have enough money? (Already the edge is off the thrill.) You've heard accommodations are hard to come by on short notice. Who will take care of the cats and water the plants? (Your mood moves lower.) Your boss will probably hassle you about time off on such short notice. Maybe she'll think you have such a lot of money that you don't need a raise. (Express elevator to low state of mind territory.) You're not so sure you want to spend a whole week with your so-called best friend. What a dumb idea! Who suggested this anyway?

The key to dealing with depressed moods is to not take the depression to heart.

We human beings are designed to be happy! Each of us goes through many different moods during a day. The one thing we can be certain of is that low moods will not last. We know from experience the mind will drop a heavy load at some point. In some cases the mind simply gets bored with the negative cycle. In others something else diverts us and we forget about it. Given the chance, the mind will integrate even the most serious tragedy in time.

This reminds me of an incident that happened to a high school friend. He was on his final solo flight in a Piper Cub. While trying a fancy maneuver at 5000 feet he found himself in a tail spin, falling to earth like a stone. He tried to fix the problem, but none of the controls had any effect. In desperation he called the control tower and asked for help. "Let go of everything! Take your hands and feet off of the controls." He did and the plane immediately righted itself -- because it's built to do that.

That's how we're built too. Stop focusing on and messing with depression and it will pass. Humor is the perfect antidote for a low mood. If you can help someone laugh a little, they'll begin to see a way out. After all, it's simply a matter of dropping the negative thoughts and the low mood is gone.

As you gain understanding for yourself, you'll begin to see more and more the natural humor in life. It will strike you as almost funny when you see people caught up in their negative thinking. But when you respond to them, you must be careful to relate out of compassionate understanding not lightly or with a feeling of superiority. If you give them your full presence, your natural optimism, and clear perspective will come through and help them drop their load -- often without any words at all. The helium principle will see to that.

The other reminder is: don't take their depression unto yourself. Your sense of well-being is your life preserver. Don't let go of it. This unfortunate customer is suffering. There is no malice here, only talk and behavior coming out of a low state of mind. It is not directed at you personally.

Everyone is drawn toward positivity and warm feelings. When you simply offer warm feelings to your customers they will respond as much as they can. But you won't help anyone by letting yourself be pulled into their private hell.

Now it's time to pull it all together and sum up....

- Peace of mind, love, and true happiness come from deep, inner positive feelings. Thus self-esteem has nothing whatsoever to do with external events. Self-esteem is lost via misunderstood thought.

24

A Few Final Thoughts for the Service Person

Customer service is simply being open and nice to people. But it has to come from a genuine warm feeling, or customers see it as insincere. If you view waiting on customers and dealing with the public in a positive light you are on your way to success.

Customers feel you are giving them fine service when you have presence. Presence is the inherent feeling of well-being all of us have when not distracted by our negative or irrelevant thoughts, judgments, or, preoccupations. It's like a light bulb in a room. As dust and spots collect on it, even blobs of mud, the light grows dimmer. Simply cleaning the surface (dropping the judgments, limiting beliefs and negative thoughts) allows the natural brightness to shine. People are drawn to this bright presence and effected in a positive way.

You will find yourself dropping negative thoughts automatically if it strikes you as a sensible thing to do. If you see that it makes good sense to stop festering on negativity, practice will enable you to catch and drop these thoughts more and more readily. At some point a negative thought in your head will begin to sound like a firecracker in a church -- totally out of place.

The hurdle we each face is our own thinking which blocks our feeling of presence. Let's summarize the major obstacles:

Habitual reactions to customer's

¤ *mannerisms, appearance and dress.*
Everyone acts and dresses in accordance with what they think, and thus see, is proper.

¤ *opinions and ways of seeing the world.*
Remember that everyone has a unique set of filters (thoughts and beliefs) through which they view the world -- each a unique culture.

¤ *moods and manners.*
When someone is in a negative frame of mind they must act with negative manner. Be understanding to those trapped in a low mood. Common sense can tell you that their entire thinking process and logic becomes negative.

Lack of understanding.

To the extent that you do not understand the power of thought, you must feel that the way you see things is the right way, the only way. This is a massive blinder to the deeper feelings. Through understanding and common sense, you get to choose between being "right" or having the nice feeling of presence.

The 'fix it' mentality.

The common mythology today says that we need to attack and get to the bottom of personal problems. This is certainly supported by psychology's pathology- and problem-centered model. Common sense says we need to learn the opposite. Don't scratch the sore, let it heal. The helium principle draws people toward a more positive state of mind, where solutions become obvious. Compassion, not confrontation, is the universal lubricant in interpersonal affairs.

If, after all of this, you look back and see that you lost your presence with a customer, and aggravated the situation, or ended up slipping into a customer's mire of despair -- forget it! You did the best you could. Next time your best will be better. That's how we all learn. The ability to forgive yourself paves the way to the nice feelings and deeper understanding. In matters of the heart, deeper feelings are the teacher. As long as you are full of nice feelings you are gaining understanding. That's just common sense.

Learning about common sense must happen via an internal realization, not by an intellectual process. As an example, a client recently said that she had grown mistrustful of her new husband. She feared that he was having an affair, although she knew it was ridiculous to harbor such thoughts. Her own insecurity was keeping her from listening to her common sense. Her filters showed her all of his actions in the most negative, suspicious way.

To help her see this we talked about other people's mindtraps. She could see that people who fear they never have enough money despite tens of thousands in the bank are trapped in a negative pattern of thought -- there's never enough. She could see that the anorexic has a self-image (thought system) that is always overweight regardless of

131

what the scales or her friends tell her. In each case the person's thought system both creates and validates their perception, so no amount of data, outside advice, or opinion can make a difference.

As we talked about insecurity and the power of compassion and understanding, this frightened wife began to uncover her deeper feelings. As her state of mind lightened, her feeling of insecurity receded, and she could see that her jealousy was unfounded, but was driving her husband away.

Her own low state of mind was in the process of bringing into reality her imagined fears.

Happily, that realization changed her state of mind, inner strength, and the way she saw everything -- and, of course, the feelings she brought to the relationship. Soon she could bring him so much unconditional love and deep feeling that now he can't wait to get back home every day.

Each of you has a wonderful opportunity to contribute something beautiful to the lives of your customers. It is a marvelous privilege. You can be a catalyst for the discovery of deeper feelings. There is a ripple effect to good feeling. When you draw others into a more positive state of mind, their entire day looks better. In turn, they will interact with their families and friends in a more positive way.

It may not seem like much at the start -- a real smile as you hand the customer his change instead of a mechanical grimace -- but a little bit works wonders in human affairs. And the bonus is that you get to live in a beautiful reality.

Being in service to other human beings is a great feeling. Egos aside, your state of mind about your job and your client and customers makes your day.

25

—

A Word To Management

Many businesses today are under increasing pressure to provide better service to their customers. Even banks and telephone companies are being forced to compete at the service level. Real estate firms are finding that the impersonal professional manner is no longer good enough. Customers in restaurants, haircutting salons, hotels and airlines demand service. Customers are going where they are treated best. In fact the only place where customers are still willing to put up with poor service today is in discount operations, and even there, where service has to be kept to an absolute minimum, competition in service at that low cost level has begun.

The retail business is beginning to become aware of this. Nordstrom, a retail department store chain out of Seattle with a well deserved reputation for top quality customer satisfaction is successfully competing with major retailers such as Macy's in the west and soon Bloomingdales in the east. Success feeds on success. Since shoppers spread the word about the wonderful service, Nordstrom can afford to spend less on advertising than its competitors and pay its employees more generously. Nordstrom promotes people instead of products.

On a recent shopping trip with my wife to one of their stores, I asked the sales woman what kind of training employees received that could lead to such excellent customer care. Without a moment's hesitation she replied, "None actually. It's just that the company treats us so well that of course we want to take good care of the company's customers."

One Nordstrom executive put it this way: "Customer service is being nice to people. You can't demand that of employees any more than you can order people to be happy. We try to create a company climate in which nice people finish first. Management's job is to support sales people. When we promote in management we may make allowances for certain shortcomings -- but never for faulty human relations skills."

Generous pay is, of course, a factor, but the sincere wish to satisify customers is an attitude that can't be bought; it must be generated from the top down. It doesn't work to order employees to treat customers well if the human relations climate within the organization is not governed by attitudes of optimism, helpfulness, presence, and concern for people. In other words, everyone in the company must truly see service as job one.

So let's say you want your sales people to make customer satisfaction their prime focus. This means the supervisors and department heads must see their primary job as serving the sales people, the middle managers must be serving supervisors, the executive committee must be serving the middle managers. The president must see his job as serving and supporting the entire staff. Even merchandising, accounting, training, and legal departments must see themselves in service. Service has to be the dominant keynote of the organization from top to bottom.

Employees' needs must and will be taken care of. If no one else pays attention to an employee's rights, salary reviews, raises, and bonuses, then the employee will. The worse the human relations climate, the more time employees spend thinking about, talking about, and looking after their personal interests. That time and attention will not be available to the customer. Like driving, if conditions are favorable, you can drive with most of your attention focused on the road ahead and respond easily to changing conditions and needs. If something worrisome happens behind you (tailgater? police car?) you will instantly direct more attention on the rearview mirror leaving less for the road ahead. Your responsiveness to changes in the traffic pattern is instantly reduced.

In organizations, insecurity drives people to the rearview mirror. The less people sense they are served and cared for by their managers, the more they will focus on taking care of themselves. These distractions automatically reduce the presence employees give to their jobs. Anyone who has flown on airlines where strikes are imminent has experienced this first hand.

Customer satisfaction has little to do with the words and gestures used. We've all been into stores where the clerks have been told to say "Thank you for shopping at .....". It has no more effect than if they had programmed the cash registers to say it. Customer satisfaction is a feeling that results from an attitude. Attitudes are determined by the way people see and think.

In the long run, every organization reflects the values, philosophy, and vision of the executive at the top. In our programs with numerous companies in different industries we have always found this to be true. For that reason, when we undertake a program to develop a customer satisfaction mentality we always start with the top level. The executives who most easily absorb this way of seeing business are those who already respect and value people highly.

Technical and financial people sometimes have a harder time understanding customer satisfaction. Their focus is often more on the intellectual. But any executive or manager can profitably learn the service attitude. It is simply a matter of helping top level people to a deeper understanding of how people really function; at some point they see their work in a new perspective and become more compassionate and understanding. It's a characteristic of human nature to want nice feeling towards people and to take pride in the work we do.

Employees are just people. They want to do a good job, and given the opportunity, they will. As a manager, it's your business to provide that opportunity.

Watch for insecurity. You want to develop a sensitive nose for the foul smell of it just as you would seek out rotting food in a corner. Insecurity brings out the worst in everyone. It shows up as politicking, indecisiveness, excessive policies and procedures, "cover myself" memos, empire building, conflict, inflexibility, and lowered creativity.

You can set the direction toward excellence by knowing, and letting your workers know you know, they are capable of producing excellence. By supporting them in this and all other ways, you will establish a climate that surpasses your wildest expectations.

When the true spirit of service permeates a company, the world quickly recognizes it, and piles success upon success.

For information on ordering products by
Robert Kausen
please see the back pages, 141-143

● Virtuous action appears to be common sense to a person in a high state of mind.

ADDITIONAL LEARNING

The reader who senses that there is more here than meets the eye may appreciate exploring the following additional resources:

Second Chance, by Syd Banks, Duval-Bibb Publishing
In Quest of the Pearl, by Syd Banks, Duval-Bibb Pub.

Sanity, Insanity, and Common Sense: The Groundbreaking New Approach to Happiness, by Suarez, Mills, and Stewart, Fawcett Columbine

Understanding, by Jane Nelsen, Prima Publishing & Communications

The Serenity Principle: Peace of Mind Through Recovery, by Joseph Bailey, Harper & Rowe

Coming Home, a collection of poems by Sue Pettit, Sunrise Press

The Quality of Life, Video Series, by Dr. George Pransky Available direct from the author. Write P.O. Box 506, La Conner, WA 98257, or call (206)466-4955.

- Creativity spawns in a relaxed, reflective state of mind. Preconception, fear, and attachment to the past inhibit the creative state.

BOOKS AND TAPES AVAILABLE

To: Life Education®, Inc.   Phone: (916) 266-3235
St. Rt. 2-3969
Trinity Center, CA 96091

BOOKS:	*Price*	*Quantity*	*Amount*
CUSTOMER SATISFACTION GUARAN-TEED: A New Approach To Customer Service, Bedside Manner, and Relation-ship Ease by Robert Kausen	$7.95	_____	_____

CASSETTE TAPES:

A WALK ON THE SOFTSIDE: Stylist's Guide to Customer & Job Satisfaction by Robert Kausen (2-Tape album with il-lustrations)	$24.95	_____	_____
SOFT SIDE MANAGEMENT FOR HARD LINE RESULTS:Salon Manager's Guide to Creating Excellence in Customer Satisfaction by Kausen (2 tape album)	$24.95	_____	_____

SUBTOTAL _____

Discount, 2 or more items, less 20%   (_____)

SUBTOTAL _____

California Residents add 6% sales tax   + _____

Shipping and handling(Book Rate)
BOOKS: $1.75 1st one   + _____
        $0.50 each additional

Make check or money   TOTAL
order payable to
Life Education, Inc.

___Check here if you would like information on programs for your business
___Check here if you would like information on residential programs in
    Coffee Creek, CA

Ship to _____
Address_____
City _____State_____Zip_____
Phone (in case we have questions on order) (___)_____

141

BOOKS AND TAPES AVAILABLE

To: Life Education®, Inc.   Phone: (916) 266-3235
St. Rt. 2-3969
Trinity Center, CA 96091

BOOKS:	Price	Quantity	Amount
CUSTOMER SATISFACTION GUARAN-TEED: A New Approach To Customer Service, Bedside Manner, and Relationship Ease by Robert Kausen	$7.95	_____	_____

CASSETTE TAPES:

	Price	Quantity	Amount
A WALK ON THE SOFTSIDE: Stylist's Guide to Customer & Job Satisfaction by Robert Kausen(2-Tape album with illustrations)	$24.95	_____	_____
SOFT SIDE MANAGEMENT FOR HARD LINE RESULTS:Salon Manager's Guide to Creating Excellence in Customer Satisfaction by Kausen (2 tape album)	$24.95	_____	_____

SUBTOTAL _____

Discount, 2 or more items, less 20%   (_____)

SUBTOTAL _____

California Residents add 6% sales tax   + _____

Shipping and handling(Book Rate)
BOOKS: $1.75 1st one   + _____
            $0.50 each additional

Make check or money   TOTAL
order payable to
Life Education, Inc.

___Check here if you would like information on programs for your business
___Check here if you would like information on residential programs in
      Coffee Creek, CA

Ship to _____
Address_____
City _____State_____Zip_____
Phone (in case we have questions on order) (__)_____

BOOKS AND TAPES AVAILABLE

To: Life Education®, Inc.   Phone: (916) 266-3235
St. Rt. 2-3969
Trinity Center, CA 96091

BOOKS:	*Price*	*Quantity*	*Amount*
CUSTOMER SATISFACTION GUARAN-TEED: A New Approach To Customer Service, Bedside Manner, and Relation-ship Ease by Robert Kausen	$7.95	_____	_____

CASSETTE TAPES:

A WALK ON THE SOFTSIDE: Stylist's Guide to Customer & Job Satisfaction by Robert Kausen(2-Tape album with il-lustrations)	$24.95	_____	_____
SOFT SIDE MANAGEMENT FOR HARD LINE RESULTS:Salon Manager's Guide to Creating Excellence in Customer Satisfaction by Kausen (2 tape album)	$24.95	_____	_____

SUBTOTAL   _____

Discount, 2 or more items, less 20%   (_____)

SUBTOTAL   _____

California Residents add 6% sales tax   + _____

Shipping and handling(Book Rate)
BOOKS: $1.75 1st one   + _____
        $0.50 each additional

Make check or money   TOTAL   ┌──────────┐
order payable to   │   │
Life Education, Inc.   └──────────┘

___Check here if you would like information on programs for your business
___Check here if you would like information on residential programs in
     Coffee Creek, CA

Ship to _____
Address_____
City _____State_____Zip_____
Phone (in case we have questions on order) (__)_____

BOOKS AND TAPES AVAILABLE

To: Life Education®, Inc.   Phone: (916) 266-3235
St. Rt. 2-3969
Trinity Center, CA 96091

BOOKS:	Price	Quantity	Amount
CUSTOMER SATISFACTION GUARAN-TEED: A New Approach To Customer Service, Bedside Manner, and Relation-ship Ease by Robert Kausen	$7.95	_____	_____

CASSETTE TAPES:

	Price	Quantity	Amount
A WALK ON THE SOFTSIDE: Stylist's Guide to Customer & Job Satisfaction by Robert Kausen(2-Tape album with il-lustrations)	$24.95	_____	_____
SOFT SIDE MANAGEMENT FOR HARD LINE RESULTS:Salon Manager's Guide to Creating Excellence in Customer Satisfaction by Kausen (2 tape album)	$24.95	_____	_____

SUBTOTAL _____

Discount, 2 or more items, less 20%   (_____)

SUBTOTAL _____

California Residents add 6% sales tax   + _____

Shipping and handling(Book Rate)
BOOKS: $1.75 1st one   + _____
          $0.50 each additional

Make check or money   TOTAL
order payable to
Life Education, Inc.

___Check here if you would like information on programs for your business
___Check here if you would like information on residential programs in
      Coffee Creek, CA

Ship to _____
Address_____
City _____State_____Zip_____
Phone (in case we have questions on order) (___)_____